Praise for *Konnect Better*

"This belongs in every home and organization that values trust, empathy, and repair."

—Marshall Goldsmith, #1 *New York Times* bestselling author of *Triggers* and *The Earned Life*

"For anyone who wants to slow down, notice more, and reconnect to what truly matters."

—Shaun Francis, chair and CEO of Medcan; author of *Eat, Move, Think: The Path to a Healthier, Stronger, Happier You*

"This book will help you understand yourself and your loved ones, and ultimately help you have a truly happier life. Read this book carefully, and your life will be imbued with more emotional intelligence and meaning."

—UJ Ramdas, cofounder of Intelligent Change, creator of *The Five Minute Journal* and the *Productivity Planner*

"Practical, actionable, and easy to read."

—Randall Craig, CEO, Braintrust Professional Institute

konnect better

unlocking the power of your relationships

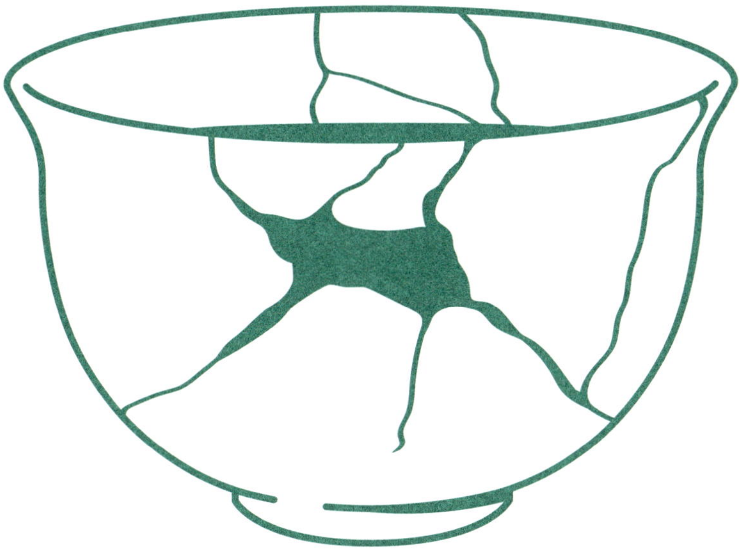

Mo Lidsky, PhD

Bob Gould

amplify

an imprint of Amplify Publishing Group

amplify
an imprint of Amplify Publishing Group

www.amplifypublishinggroup.com

Konnect Better: Unlocking the Power of Your Relationships (Volume One: Committed Connections)

For more information, please contact:
Amplify Publishing, an imprint of Amplify Publishing Group
620 Herndon Parkway, Suite 220
Herndon, VA 20170
info@amplifypublishing.com

Library of Congress Control Number: 2025909812

CPSIA Code: PRV0925A

ISBN-13: 979-8-89138-579-5

Printed in the United States

Dedicated to the spouses, partners, children, parents, and friends who endured us for the many years it took to appreciate the preciousness of these relationships, and how much our words, thoughts, and actions need to be adjusted to reflect that appreciation.

CONTENTS

Section Two

Action

This section is about developing skills for navigating and nurturing relationships, such as mastering emotions, making effective requests, and managing and adapting our behaviors for stronger, healthier connections.

Chapters

Section Three
Alignment

In this final section, learn how to align efforts for long-term growth, deepen emotional and physical intimacy, and maintain a healthy balance in the relationship. This will include tools for fostering harmony, intimacy, growth, and lasting connection over time.

Chapters

Preface

THERE'S NO GREATER JOY for Canadians than waking up to warmth. Watching the Playa del Carmen sunrise from my balcony, I couldn't help but feel immense gratitude for the beauty and privilege surrounding me, my family, my health, and my business. Yet this quiet moment of reflection stirred a deeper question: Am I truly giving back enough to the world that has given so much to me? Sure, I've been involved with countless charitable causes and generally try to live a socially conscious existence, but the ocean sounds inspired me to think bigger. What would it take to make a real dent in the universe?

I began contemplating the possibilities. What's the greatest gift I could bestow on as many people as possible? If I were to give something to a billion people to truly impact their lives, what would it be? The more I thought about it, the more it occurred to me that nothing physical would do the trick. Any object that you could give to a billion people would have limited long-term benefits for most of them. Infusing their lives with newfound joy would require something intangible. But what? I was committed to using my beachfront laboratory to figure it out.

For the next three days, as I sat at my resort's cabana where various unwitting poor souls occupied the chairs and cabanas around me, I proceeded to ask all of them the same question.

[If you were on a stage with a podium and had eight billion of the world's population in front of you, what would you say to them to improve their lives?]

Notwithstanding the many raised eyebrows, surprisingly, most people tolerated my eccentricity. No one told me to fly a kite, and dozens indulged my curiosity by sharing their thoughts.

The responses ranged from the mundane ("Spend more time with your family") to the bizarre ("Get closer to people who are as weird as you") to the proselytizing ("Strengthen your relationship with the Lord"). I collected and recorded over thirty responses and spent my last day in Mexico finding a running theme among all of them. The answer was clear as day. Everyone claimed that life could be improved by "strengthening your relationship with ______." The blank can be a spouse, parents, God, self, friends, kids, community, or nature. It doesn't matter whom or what we're talking about, but somehow a focus on nurturing those intangible connections seemed to be the unanimous choice for an improved life.

I left Mexico committed to changing the world. And did absolutely nothing about it.

A year later, returning to a similar spot, I reflected on the last decade of building my firm. My partners and I spent many years helping ultra-high-net-worth families increase the probability of achieving a specific rate of return. We believed that this was how we could add value. Though, after more than a decade of delivering on our promises, I realized that we achieved the mandate but not the goal. All our clients were happy with us, but they weren't necessarily happier people. We hit the numbers but didn't profoundly improve their lives.

As calming waves were crashing down in front of me, the seemingly obvious epiphany hit me like a ton of bricks. For truly affluent individuals, with many millions (if not billions), what difference would a 13 percent rate of return make versus an 11 percent, or 9 percent, or 7 percent rate of return? Yes, there is the fun of the game or the desire to do anything well. And yes, you can do more when there is more. Though, ultimately, how will incremental returns improve the lives of asset owners and beneficiaries? In most cases, the answer is not much. Conversely, there's a huge benefit from incremental love.

So I reflected on the previous Mexico trip and realized that the answer was staring me in the face. What mattered to the .01 percent of the population was no different than what mattered to the remaining 99.99 percent. The intangibles would improve everyone's life. The only difference was that the ultra-affluent could do so at higher levels of Maslow's hierarchy.* They could dabble more in self-actualization through philanthropy, intergenerational legacies, and the luxury of time. Though to get there,

* Maslow's hierarchy is a psychological theory that outlines a five-level model of human needs, with each level in the hierarchy often depicted within a pyramid. At the bottom of the hierarchy, we have our most basic physiological needs (food, water, shelter), the next level up being safety and security needs (job, health, protection), the level above that being love and belonging needs (family, friends, community), the level above that being self-esteem (confidence, achievement, respect), and the highest level being self-actualization (purpose, creativity, morality). Typically, one needs to satisfy the lower needs before they can attend to the higher needs.

they must satisfy their need for community, belonging, love, family, and intimacy—and many people never do.

I left Mexico and recommitted to changing the world. Beyond achieving superior returns and resilient portfolios, I wanted to help our families improve their lives and relationships. And once again, I did absolutely nothing.

For the next twelve months, which included the COVID-19 chaos of 2020, one of my few constants was a weekly call with Bob Gould. Bob has spent the last thirty years helping Canada's most influential families protect that which they care about most, have the conversations they need to have, and achieve the harmony they crave. My relationship with Bob started with his mentorship and collaborative work on families but ultimately evolved into a sacred and trusting friendship.

Our weekly chats were free-flowing and often philosophical but always anchored on the human condition. We frequently delved into common mistakes and best practices; we discussed how people show up, what they genuinely want to take care of, and where so many miss the mark. We consistently challenged each other with the perennial question of what our role is with those around us, how we express it in our day jobs, and where we should focus our resources.

One December morning at 4:19 a.m., I received an email from Bob with the subject line, "Eureka!" In it, he cryptically said, "Mo, I think I've finally put it together… how we can move the needle in this world… what is the one thing we all want?" It took a follow-up email for Bob to announce his revelation: "To get closer!"

By the time Bob comically serenaded me with Seals and Crofts's 1976 version of "Get Closer," I had heard enough. What followed were countless calls and conversations, seeking the advice of experts, and debating how we can collaborate to help people get closer, to strengthen their relationships with ______ (fill in the blank), and to make a positive dent in our universe. While we had at least as many questions as we had answers, with Bob's decades of experience in family dynamics at my side, it was all the impetus I needed to get started.

Now that I had the perfect partner and I'd exhausted all my excuses, I was ready to work on building konnect better. And it's through that work that this book was born.

As you embark on this journey with us, my only hope is that this book will have the transformative impact on your life that it had on mine.

—Mo Lidsky

Introduction

I WILL FOREVER CARRY THE MEMORY of Mark's piercing gaze as he uttered, "I wish it wasn't you sitting here with me." The profound sadness in his eyes penetrated my soul. It wasn't an insult; it was an authentic expression of lament and acceptance of his fate.

Mark* was anything but ordinary. His business empire was so vast that his net worth surpassed the combined GDP of Madagascar, Somalia, Sudan, and Yemen. He was regarded as a trailblazer in his field, with an extensive portfolio of extraordinary assets worldwide. He had employed tens of thousands. Yet on his deathbed, it was just the two of us. The profound sadness I felt in that moment must have paled in comparison to his.

Mark's romantic life was a series of unsuccessful attempts to find true love, cycling through several spouses. Despite having children, he struggled to form a conventional parental bond with any of them. Countless friends and contacts surrounded him, but he lacked intimate connections. He indulged in every conceivable

---

* The name and some identifying details have been changed to protect the privacy of the individual involved.

luxury, partied with women worldwide, and dabbled in philanthropy. Nevertheless, here he was, confiding in me that his life felt like he had built mansions on quicksand, futile investments in a futile life.

Over the years, Mark would frequently tell me that no one could be trusted. He suspected everyone—be they romantic partners, employees, family members, or friends (including me)—was only interested in his wealth. Mark's subconscious belief that he was unworthy of love prevented him from truly experiencing it.

In my efforts to help Mark finally "settle down," I introduced him to remarkable women. His charismatic charm would secure him second, third, or even fourth dates. However, inevitably, his narcissism, stubbornness, and Napoleon complex would surface. To romantic partners, he was emotionally unavailable; to his children, incorrigible; to "friends," a curmudgeon; and to his employees, a volatile eccentric (albeit a well-paying one).

To Mark, there was no problem for which "money" wasn't a solution. To the outside observer, there was no situation where it wasn't part of the problem. As Mark once depressingly put it, "No one calls me unless they need my money."

So at this moment, death stared him in the face. All the family members had been notified, and there were no more calls to be made. Yet it was just the two of us, with Mark sorrowfully grumbling, "I wish it wasn't you sitting here with me . . . I wish I knew how to do it right."

In my business, I have the privilege of advising some of North America's most affluent families on how to optimally allocate their capital. These individuals possess intergenerational wealth that will outlive them. For ultra-affluent individuals, the practice of compounding capital that will live on beyond their lifetimes is well entrenched.* However, the idea of compounding the quality of their relationships may not receive the same attention. It is remarkable that these individuals, who won't let money sit idle for a moment, often allow their important relationships to stagnate or even deteriorate over time.

Even more astonishingly, I have witnessed many individuals who have strained relationships with their children willing to give up most, if not all, of their wealth to mend those broken bonds. Similarly, those grappling with failing health would give up almost everything to regain it. Yet these same individuals will neglect to proactively invest in their relationships, despite the undeniable correlation between relationship strength and overall health.

Extensive research has consistently demonstrated the profound impact of relationships on one's health. Studies revealed that men who frequently used first-person pronouns like "I," "me," and "mine" (rather than "we," "us," and "our") were more susceptible to heart disease and heart attacks.[1] In a separate study involving twenty-three hundred heart attack survivors, social connectedness had a greater influence on survival rate than the medications respondents took, the diets they maintained, and even whether they consumed alcohol or smoked.[2]

A study conducted of seven thousand Californians showed that those with weak relationships were three times more likely to die within the decade of the study.[3] In fact, a meta review of more recent studies on mortality rates reaffirms the correlation

---

* In *Frank Lloyd Wright on Architecture: Selected Writings, 1894–1940* (1941), Wright comically observed, "[I don't understand why] many wealthy people are [satisfied being] little more than the janitors of their possessions."

between stronger relationships and longevity.[4] Those with stronger connections have reduced risk of cardiovascular disease. Conversely, those with poor social relationships have a 29 percent increased risk of coronary heart disease and a 32 percent increased risk for stroke.[5]

All these studies suggest the importance of prioritizing the strength of our relationships over our material assets. In fact, for many individuals like myself, who faced socioeconomic hardship growing up, the emotional bonds and care provided by a parent often outweigh the fulfillment of even basic physiological needs. Yet despite living in the most prosperous and abundant era in history, our relationships still don't receive the attention and importance they deserve. Many of us wish to improve them but don't have the tools to do so. Instead, we stumble through our attempts, sometimes straining relationships with those who are close but could be so much closer. And since each of us can "konnect better," I hope this book can serve as a valuable resource.

Despite the overwhelming evidence that relationships are critically important to health, success, and happiness, none of our social institutions teach us how to manage them. Our educational systems don't teach us how to effectively navigate various facets of our lives—personal, professional, spiritual, social, and familial—in ways that truly work. We are taught basic manners, like saying "please" and "thank you," but not how to understand the very diverse styles of communication that exist across the human spectrum. We learn how to express disappointment or frustration, but not how to reconcile conflicting expectations.

We are taught to use social media and technology, but not how to adapt our primal instincts to the fast-changing world with a flood of information. We know how to accumulate wealth and attain power, but not how to convert it into lasting happiness, meaning, and fulfillment. We have been conditioned to pursue "more" but have not learned what is "enough." We have learned how to connect with others, but not how to get closer to them.

The result of these educational gaps is evident. While we have witnessed increased wealth levels, improved access to health care and social services, higher levels of education, and even the eradication of poverty in some regions, happiness has not increased correspondingly, and mental health challenges are at all-time highs.

In 1974, a study conducted by University of Pennsylvania professor Richard Easterlin highlighted this happiness dynamic in a study known as the Easterlin Paradox. The study posited that a nation's economic growth does not necessarily lead to an increase in overall happiness. For example, in the United States, real incomes have tripled over the past seven decades, but Americans have experienced zero to negative increases in the levels of aggregate happiness.[6] Similar patterns have been identified in other developed and developing countries. The pursuit of economic expansion and the hedonic treadmill often associated with it have kept our happiness levels standing in place.

So What's the Solution, and How Do We Achieve More Happiness?

The study of human happiness has been a timeless pursuit. More than two and a half millennia ago, Socrates criticized the Athenians for prioritizing the pursuit of wealth and hedonistic pleasure over the pursuit of fulfillment and eudaemonia—the true nourishment of the soul.

Fast-forward a couple of thousand years to 1938, and you'd find Harvard University recruiting 268 students to examine what constitutes a happy and healthy life.[7] This study, which has evolved into the longest-running study on adult development, has continued for more than eighty-five years, with a small fraction of the original cohort alive today.[8] The initial participants, who experienced the hardships of the Great Depression, were followed throughout their lives. Subsequent generations and a control group of inner-city participants were included, and hundreds were added to the research over time. The study has analyzed millions of data points, and one theme has consistently emerged. Surprisingly, none of the things we generally toil for (e.g., wealth, fame, social standing, sculpted bodies, elevated education, and superior IQ) yielded as much happiness as close relationships. Nothing else proved to be as directly correlated with long-term happiness and well-being.

Close relationships did more than increase happiness levels. They also enhanced resilience to physical and mental deterioration.[9] The strength of our relationships with family and friends has a significant correlation with longevity and brain health. Conversely, loneliness and high-conflict relationships have proven to be as detrimental to our minds and bodies as alcoholism and smoking.

Interestingly, other pursuits, such as money, sex, and fame, tend to follow a happiness curve that plateaus over time. Initial doses yield an increase in happiness, with subsequent doses experiencing diminishing to no returns.[10] However, relationships are not subject to the same hedonic treadmill or adaptation. Grandparents cherish the thousandth hug from their grandkids as much as the first. The moral support of a spouse, partner, or parent with whom one can be truly vulnerable never loses its value.

In his book *Brain Rules for Aging Well*, Dr. John Medina asserts that those who engage most with their closest relationships experience a rate of cognitive decline that is 70 percent lower than those who socialize the least.

The bottom line is that there is nothing more valuable for healthy aging and life satisfaction than strong relationships.

If this is true, why don't we prioritize the need to strengthen our relationships over making money, working out, or building superficial connections on social media? Why do 72 percent of us have at least one frustrating but important relationship, either at work or at home?[11] Why do communication gaps and trust issues account for 85 percent of failures in families attempting to transition businesses to the next generation?[12]

What prevents most of us from tapping into this foundation of fulfillment? What obstacles supersede the countless benefits that emerge from close relationships and stronger communities?

What Stands in Our Way?

As the cartoonist Walt Kelly described our treatment of the environment, "We have met the enemy, and he is us."[13] Whether consciously or not, we often hinder the very relationships that could transform our lives. Why do we do that? It is not intentional. It is simply a result of the three powerful undercurrents present in every relationship: personal, interpersonal, and environmental dynamics.

Personal dynamics include the traits, tendencies, behaviors, and beliefs we bring to our relationships. These may manifest themselves as jealousy or joy, anger or compassion, pessimism or optimism, self-centeredness or selflessness. Each of these characteristics influences how we communicate with the world around us and with those we cherish most.

Interpersonal dynamics arise from the crosscurrent and collision of different people coming from diverse backgrounds. This blend of historical, psychological, and cultural elements has the potential to create magic, enabling us to benefit from the experiences, perspectives, strengths, and sensitivities of others. But if differing experiences cause people to disagree or misunderstand each other, interpersonal dynamics can introduce tensions and conflicts. Whether these conflicts strengthen or damage our relationships is often our choice to make.

Environmental dynamics encapsulate all aspects of our circumstances. They may involve the family or culture we were born into, the expectations of our community, or the various distractions clouding our relationships (e.g., technology, hobbies, work, etc.). They encompass what we have been taught about relationships, the examples we've seen, and our own misguided beliefs. Our environment sets the stage for how we connect.

In essence, relationships are challenging because we need to interpret signals from three different antennae simultaneously. First, we must recognize how we are shaped by our environment. Second, we must understand how we show up and the impact of our personal dynamics. Third, we must consider the experiences, viewpoints, and expectations of the other person, while understanding how all these factors intertwine.

Attempting to meaningfully guide people toward closer relationships across all three dimensions simultaneously is a monumental task for any book. So we'll attempt to dissect these dimensions through the three corresponding ingredients of all exceptional relationships: Committed Connections, Caring Communication, and Constructive Conflict.

- **Committed Connections** will focus on the "environmental" factors that need to be in place for any relationship to thrive. We will explore the values, principles, and foundational rules of engagement that are often left unarticulated.

- **Caring Communication** will delve into the "personal" principles and best practices that foster trusting, respectful, and effective communication. We will cover how to mitigate any potentially adverse ramifications from our diverse communication styles, limiting friction and enabling quality connection.

- **Constructive Conflict** will address how to preserve and improve relationships when they encounter inevitable rough waters, as all interpersonal dynamics do. We will explore strategies for protecting the emotional safety of those who are navigating conflicts, moving them toward better outcomes.

While these three ingredients—Committed Connections, Caring Communication, and Constructive Conflict—are not exhaustive, they cover a significant swath of relationship issues.

At first glance, these concepts may seem obvious. If you were to ask anyone what they value in a relationship, they would likely mention trust or respect or good communication. Yet many still find themselves struggling to cultivate these important relationship building blocks.

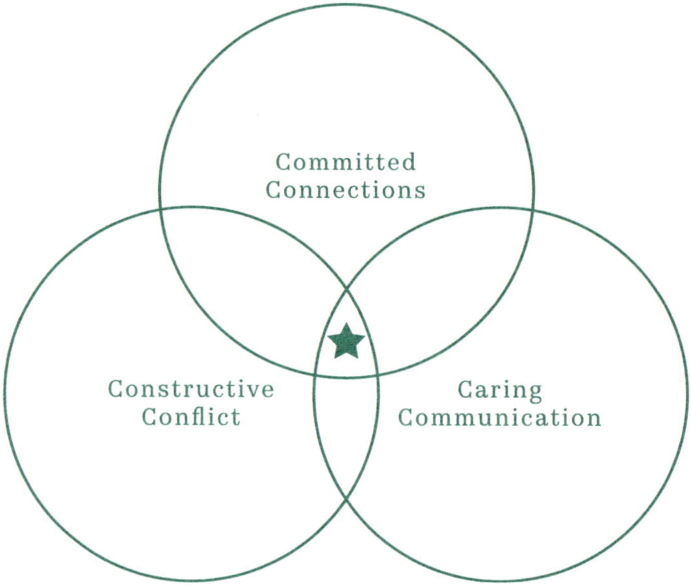

The reason for frustration lies in the fact that topics like "communication" are not simplistic or one-dimensional. They involve various components, paradigms, best practices, and common mistakes. Achieving effective communication requires understanding these frameworks and making a conscious effort to implement them in our lives.

Having great relationships involves *creating* great relationships. This, in turn, requires understanding these three building blocks and how to strike a healthy balance between them. Most healthy relationships live at the intersection of Committed Connections, Caring Communication, and Constructive Conflict.

This is one investment Mark never made. As a result, he passed away wishing he had known "how to do it right." Mark's opportunity may be gone, but by understanding the strategies, frameworks, and tactics in this book, we can still make our own investments in fostering healthier and stronger relationships, ultimately leading to far more fulfilling lives.

Our Guarantee

There are countless books and resources on relationships, and it's important to find what works best for you. The key is to actively engage in practices that enhance and deepen relationships over time. Having almost any mental model or framework to support our relationships is better than having none. Frameworks help us move away from operating on autopilot and defaulting to instinctive habits. But it's critically important to put those frameworks into practice, moving from theory to action.

This book is the culmination of decades of observation. Studying relationships that didn't work, studying those that did, and benefiting from the wisdom of numerous relationship experts.

I have such conviction in the tools within this book that I guarantee they will make a tangible difference in your relationships. If you diligently apply the tools provided—by patiently digesting the contents, reflecting on them, and actively practicing the exercises—your relationships (at least those that aren't toxic and unhealable)* will improve. This book will not solve all your interpersonal problems, and your relationships won't be perfect, even if you master and apply the tools offered, but you will experience better connections with those who matter most to you.

We are so confident in these practices that we are willing to offer a guarantee. If you follow our recommendations and don't feel it helped your relationship, we will refund you your money in full.

Yes, you heard correctly. We are prepared to make this guarantee because we truly believe in the effectiveness of these tools. However, this assurance is contingent upon you doing your part. It requires your active participation.

Within this first volume of the series, you will find seventeen short chapters, but we would encourage you to go through them slowly, as you will want to properly digest, practice, and embody these ideas. Take the time to let the content sink in, and remember that true learning comes from active practice, not intellectual comprehension of ideas. Try to maintain some consistency in reviewing the content, employing the exercises, and taking full advantage of the supporting reference tools. We can provide you with the frameworks, but only you can put in the work.

It's worth noting that the relationships covered in this book extend beyond romantic, commercial, or familial ones. They encompass *any type of relationship with any number of individuals.* Examples and tools may be drawn from various domains. Furthermore, some tactics may work better in one context than another.

---

* We will cover unsalvageable relationships in the chapter on last efforts and limits in volume 3. While there are some relationships that are beyond repair, making that determination requires careful thought and consideration.

Yet all the tools and frameworks provided in this book offer a useful mental model for nurturing your "North Star Relationship."

Our North Star

Before you embark on this journey, it's crucial to center our attention on the ultimate objective and clearly identify the specific relationship(s) you desire to improve. Take a moment to reflect and write down the name(s) of the individual(s) with whom you most want to enhance your relationship(s). This could include a family member, spouse, friend, colleague, or even multiple people within a specific area of your life. If there are additional relationships you'd like to focus on, please use the extra space below to list them.

This year, I'm going to improve my relationship with . . .

____

____

____

____

This will serve as your *North Star Relationship (NSR)*, which will act as your point of focus throughout this book. Whenever we mention the NSR, simply substitute it with the specific relationship you've chosen to focus on, be it your spouse, partner, sibling, child, parent, friend, or any other you've prioritized to improve.

Before diving deeper, it's important to assess the current

state of your chosen relationship. In Appendix I, you'll find a helpful tool called "the Relationship Assessment Scale," which will assist you in this process. It can also be accessed online at *konnectbetter.com* or through *the konnect better app.*

Remember, a low satisfaction score on the Relationship Assessment Scale doesn't necessarily mean you should give up on the relationship. It may indicate that more effort is required to improve it. Similarly, a high satisfaction score does not preclude anyone from increasing the benefit of their NSR. The assessment is merely a starting point for your journey and a baseline from which to gauge future progress.

Many of our relationships have the potential to bring greater joy, pleasure, and fulfillment into our lives. However, they can also bring moments of heartache, disappointment, and frustration. Our aim is for the remaining chapters of this book to unlock the potential for enhancing your NSR and creating a more meaningful and fulfilling connection.

We wish you an enjoyable and transformative journey ahead!

section one
AWARENESS

Collapsing Cox Industries: A Story of the Missing Connection

It is hard to imagine someone less self-aware than Alexander "Alex" Cox. Alex was the beneficiary of a third-generation industrial business, built by his immigrant grandfather and stewarded successfully by his father. When the business was bestowed on Alex and his two sisters, Caroline and Helena, they had factories around the world and industry-leading technology, generating over $330 million of free cash flow with a bright future ahead.

Sadly, the three siblings had a relationship that was so fragmented, they couldn't agree on whether it was day or night. They fought relentlessly, almost jeopardizing the business on two occasions. Thankfully, the previous generation put in place such a strong management team and organizational culture that the company endured. Eventually, Alex bought out his sisters. The transaction was acrimonious, leading Alex to have virtually no contact with his sisters for almost a decade. Even the invitations to both of his sons' destination weddings were intentionally delivered at the last minute to decrease the likelihood of their attendance.

Alex's two sons, Nick and Chris, were accomplished professionals—a professor and an engineer working outside the business. Having seen the perils of the previous generation, they wanted no part of it. However, when Alex began experiencing health issues, he informed his sons that he expected them to step in. Of course, they had no interest in either the business or working with their father. Yet after Alex's relentless guilt trips, their mother's pressure tactics, and even bribing the boys' spouses by offering extraordinary financial incentives (a base salary of

$1.5 million for each of the sons, which was orders of magnitude greater than their earning potential in the market), eventually, Nick and Chris reluctantly agreed. Of course, they had no idea that this massive upgrade in lifestyle would be accompanied by a massive downgrade in joy. Alex started to lord this financial arrangement over the boys and threatened them at the slightest sign of disobedience.

Within one year, Alex's relationships with his sons had deteriorated. From the outset, there was no clarity about how their new boss-employee dynamic would work. They did not know when they could lean on him as a father or when he would show up as a demanding manager. There was no clarity on what agency they had, and despite their many requests, there was no clear job description.

While Alex was focused on preserving his legacy, Nick and Chris were drinking from a firehose, trying to learn, adapt, and tolerate their father's incessant berating. They felt disrespected and not trusted, and all attempts to communicate their feelings to Alex were largely ignored. Worse yet, Alex often retaliated with threats, guilt trips, and angry blow-ups. Control was Alex's only currency. Discussions of emotions were now nonexistent, and the sons were forced to employ tactics to navigate around their father, as there was no changing his behavior. Eventually all communication ceased, family gatherings were abandoned, and it wasn't long until all conversations required lawyers around the table. The prospect of reconciliation or Committed Connections was gone.

After Chris started experiencing panic attacks and Nick's marriage almost collapsed, both sons submitted their resignations, without a single discussion with their father—despite threats of being excluded from the wills. They downsized their lifestyles, moved away, and never uttered another word to Alex again. Six years later, Alex was sued by his employees and vendors and defaulted on his debt payments, and the business was declared bankrupt. Alex spent the remaining four years of his life in court, without ever meeting two of his newborn grandchildren.

This Cox family story is a powerful reminder of the critical need for Committed Connections. And it's important to clarify what we mean by examining these words individually: *committed* and *connection*.

Committed signifies the ability to maintain a long-term perspective in a relationship, regardless of the challenges that may arise. Commitment connotes a covenantal, rather than transactional, relationship. It involves making decisions and taking actions based on what is best for the relationship, rather than solely focusing on your individual needs. Committed individuals are willing to make sacrifices and extend themselves without expecting immediate reciprocity.

Connection highlights the quality of a relationship. Psychologist Melanie Joy identifies eight dimensions of connection: emotional, intellectual, psychological, sexual, physical, romantic, practical, and philosophical.[14] While most relationships can have various types and levels of connection, an emotional bond serves as the foundation for a "Committed Connection." The strength of commitment to others is most profound when we feel it at a deep, intrinsic level within ourselves. And it all starts with self-awareness.

chapter one

Self-Awareness

The first principle is that you must not fool yourself—and you are the easiest person to fool.

—Richard Feynman

HAVE YOU EVER CAUGHT YOURSELF in the middle of a rant about someone else's flaws and realized you were describing yourself? Yeah, me too. Self-awareness is like that uninvited guest who shows up at every party you throw—always with something inconveniently true to say. And while it's tempting to ignore, it's the key to unlocking our best relationships, both personal and professional.

Why Self-Awareness Matters More Than IQ

In 2009, researchers from Cornell University conducted a study titled "What Predicts Executive Success?" They followed seventy-two senior executives leading companies with annual revenues ranging from $50 million to $5 billion. The results were surprising:

intelligence, experience, and business acumen weren't the key factors determining performance. The strongest predictor of overall success among these executives was—wait for it—self-awareness.[15]

Why is self-awareness so crucial? Because leadership, at its core, is about people: managing, fostering trust, understanding how to inspire others, and bringing out the best in them. None of this happens without first understanding ourselves.

Relationship problems are rarely due to inferior intelligence. We often see simple people with modest backgrounds who have beautiful relationships, while some brilliant and successful individuals struggle in dysfunctional ones. And it's not about age or experience either—you can find young people with exceptional relationships and older folks who are still trying to figure it out.

The Power of Spotting Your Blind Spots

Relationship challenges often arise from blind spots—those parts of ourselves we can't quite see. We might not fully grasp how others interpret our actions, intentions, or emotions. And let's be honest: we're usually terrible at guessing what's going on in other people's heads.

Psychologist Daniel Goleman, known for his work on emotional intelligence, emphasizes that self-awareness is the cornerstone of strong relationships. He breaks it down into three main forms:

- ***Recognizing and understanding our own emotions:*** How do your moods impact your interactions with others?*

---

*This requires us to cultivate our ability to correctly identify, name, and monitor our emotions. This is further covered in the chapter on emotional fluency.

- ***Accurately assessing our strengths and weaknesses:*** Know thyself—and not just the LinkedIn version.

- ***Understanding your self-confidence and self-worth:*** How do you really see yourself, beyond the filters?

Self-awareness isn't just a "nice-to-have." It's your personal GPS. Without it, you might think you're headed north, but you could be driving in circles. And as with any GPS, it helps if you actually listen to it.

How to Develop Self-Awareness (without Turning into a Navel-Gazer)

In the mid-1900s, Joseph Luft and Harrington Ingham introduced a concept known as Johari's window,* which offers insight into different aspects of our identity.[16] Imagine a window with four panes:

- **Open Area:** Known to both you and others. This is the part everyone sees.

- **Blind Spot:** Known to others, but not to you. This is where feedback is gold.

- **Hidden Area:** Known to you, but hidden from others. Vulnerability unlocks this room.

* So called, as it used the amalgamation of Joseph's and Harrington's first names, "Jo" and "Hari."

- **Unknown Area:** Unknown to both you and others. The great mystery of self-discovery.

While Room Four might be a lifelong journey, all our relationships can quickly reveal the mysteries of Room Two, and trust can be deepened by disclosing the contents of Room Three.* As psychotherapist Modya Silver once shared with me, "The role of self-discovery is to build greater awareness. With more awareness, we have more choice and more freedom." Paradoxically, building more trusting relationships reduces our blind spots.

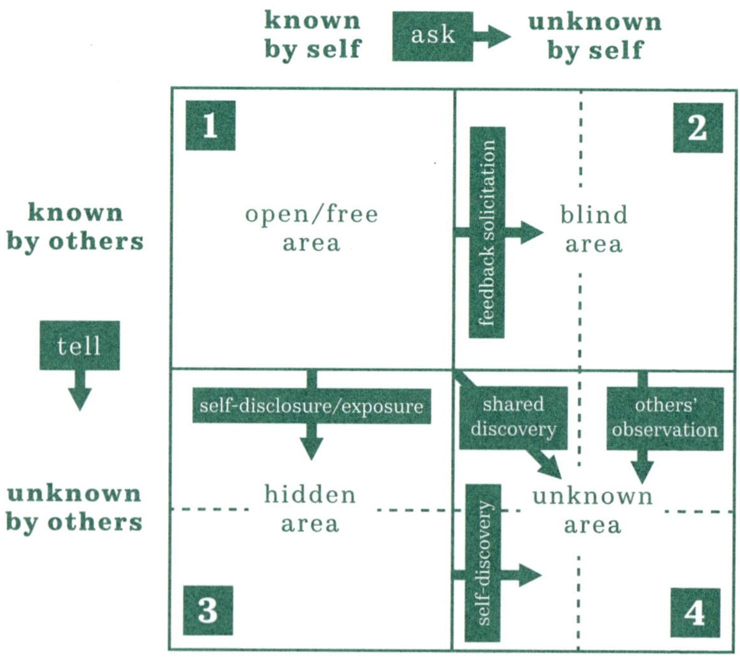

* Johari's window is merely one framework for thinking about self-awareness. There are many other tools and methods that can actually help us develop better self-awareness of our values (e.g., Enneagram), how we process information or communicate (e.g., Myers–Briggs and DiSC), and how we show up for others (e.g., Kolbe), etc.

Self-Awareness: The Relationship Superpower

Think of self-awareness as your superhero cape. When you wear it, you can dynamically manage yourself and, consequently, your relationships. But when you're not aware, it's like wearing your cape backward—you'll trip over it, and so will everyone around you.

Our relationship with ourselves is the longest one we'll ever have. Self-awareness shapes how we feel, act, react, and, ultimately, how we impact those around us. The good news? Expanding your self-awareness can start today.

Chapter Takeaways

- Self-awareness is the foundation of trust and connection. Without it, we're flying blind.
- Understand your emotions, strengths, and self-worth. It's not just about knowing your flaws—celebrate your strengths too.
- Share and listen. Vulnerability in sharing (Room Three) and openness to feedback (Room Two) shrinks your blind spots.

Following each chapter, you will find corresponding exercises as well as supplemental readings. *These will also be available online at konnectbetter.com and on the konnect better app.* These are designed to help you apply the concepts discussed in the chapter.

Remember: there's no progress without practice. Knowledge alone won't create the changes you're looking for. Real change requires experimentation, reflection, refinement, and repetition. These exercises offer you the opportunity to do so.

Exercise

Begin the process of self-discovery by reflecting on and answering one of the questions on the next page. If you can, encourage your NSR to do the same. Additional worksheets are available at konnectbetter.com.

Once complete, sit down with your NSR and take turns sharing your responses. Go through your responses uninterrupted. Regardless of what the responses may be, ensure that you thank each other for sharing and being honest. Then, allow yourself some time to ask clarifying questions. Thank them again for their transparency and willingness to do this with you.

Self-reflection	Your description	Your NSR's description*
How would you describe yourself to others without mentioning anything external to you (e.g., don't mention your profession, where you live, who your family and friends are, your hobbies, etc.)?		
What positive qualities and characteristics do you perceive yourself to have?		

*This would ideally include asking your NSR and engaging in this conversation with them. Though, in the event that's not feasible, the mere act of considering their views and prospective responses will inspire greater self-awareness.

Self-reflection	Your description	Your NSR's description
What negative qualities and characteristics do you perceive yourself to have?		
What qualities and characteristics do you not show or reveal to anyone (or hardly anyone)?		
What are the best ways to communicate with you?		
What are the ways not to communicate with you (unless you want to damage the relationship)?		
Black-belt questions for those wanting to go a couple of levels deeper.		
What do you wish you knew about yourself?		
What do you want your NSR to know that you don't often (or ever) reveal?		

Further Readings and Resources

- ***Self-Awareness:*** *The Hidden Driver of Success and Satisfaction,* by Travis Bradberry
- ***Insight:*** *The Power of Self-Awareness in a Self-Deluded World,* by Tasha Eurich

chapter two

The Ideal

If you don't know where you're going, you might wind up somewhere else.

—Yogi Berra

IMAGINE WHAT IT MIGHT BE LIKE to assemble IKEA furniture without the instructions. That's what it's like navigating relationships without knowing what you want from them—frustrating, confusing, and often ending in a slightly wonky result.

Sir John Franklin learned this the hard way on his ill-fated Arctic expedition in the 1840s. He and his crew set off to find a navigable route to Asia with no clear destination and ended up lost, unprepared, and, well . . . frozen (to death). It's a harsh reminder that wandering aimlessly, even with good intentions, doesn't end well.

In relationships, it's the same story. If we don't have a clear idea of what our ideal relationship looks like, we're likely to wind up "somewhere else"—and not in a good way. So let's chart a course.

Finding Your Ideal: Where Are You Headed?

Think of your ideal relationship like planning a road trip. You need to know your starting point (hello, Relationship Assessment Scale!) and where you're headed. No GPS can get you there without both. To get you thinking about your ideal NSR, consider:

- What does it look like? Picture your ideal relationship. How do you interact? How often? Is it like clockwork, or are you winging it? Visualize it vividly—like you're writing your own movie.

- How does it feel? What emotions would it evoke? Do you feel heard, supported, energized? What negative feelings do you want to drop-kick out the door?

- What does it bring to your life? Does this relationship connect you to your community or inspire growth? Is it your daily dose of sanity or your push to try something new? Define the "why."

Busting the Myths of the Ideal

The reality is your ideal relationship won't be a picture-perfect fairy tale. Forget grand gestures or perfect harmony twenty-four seven. More often, it's the simple stuff that counts, like being able to trust someone, feeling comfortable enough to be your weird self, and knowing they've got your back. It's about building a relationship that feels right for you, not one that looks good on social media.

Remember, there's no universal blueprint for the perfect relationship. Your ideal is unique, and it will still have some unique flaws, but that's what makes it valuable.

On the cover of this book, you'll notice a sculpted bowl created by a Japanese Kintsugi artist. Kintsugi, meaning "golden mend," is an art form that repairs broken pottery and elegantly highlights the mended areas with gold. Kintsugi embodies the philosophy of celebrating our imperfections, as they are uniquely us. While it's important to address whatever isn't working in our relationships, we must also accept and value the imperfections that shape us.

Like our Kintsugi bowl, we all have our cracks, but we become stronger and more beautiful as a result of the repairs we make. Our job isn't necessarily to smooth over every flaw, but to appreciate the gold in the seams.

Grounding Your Ideal in Reality

Before you start imagining your ideal relationship solving all your problems, let's ground it a bit. Relationships aren't destinations—you never really "arrive." They're ongoing, evolving, and sometimes messy journeys. The goal isn't perfection; it's progress, fulfillment, and joy along the way.

And remember: relationships aren't meant to "complete you." That line works in movies but not in real life. Healthy relationships start with two whole people coming together, not two halves trying to make a whole. So bring your best self, because often, our relationships reflect more about us than we like to admit.

Let's Chart Your Course

So, what does your ideal NSR look like? Take a moment to jot it down. Forget perfection, just start. Here's a quick example:

> *"An ideal relationship for me would involve more trust, friendship, and collaboration with my brother. If we had this, family gatherings would be more fun, our children would be closer, and we'd work better together in our family business. I want to rebuild a friendship with him."*

Now it's your turn. Be honest, be specific, and, most importantly, be hopeful.

What would your ideal NSR look like?

____

____

____

____

Next, we acknowledge that identifying "the ideal" also requires us to identify the obstacles that stand in the way of our ideal. Try to focus on the obstacles that are in your control to address, rather than increasing expectations of, or laying blame on, others.

Consider the issues that might impede you from reaching your NSR's potential. Is there an external environment influencing the relationship? Is there something within yourself that needs attention? Or perhaps there is a recurring pattern of behavior that requires revaluation? Take a moment to write down your thoughts. Here's another quick example:

> *"What stands in the way is my brother's resentment over the CEO role going to me despite him being older. He has harbored negative feelings toward me ever since. He frequently criticizes aspects of my lifestyle or personal choices and assumes that I am always trying to undermine him. I've also never found a healthy way to communicate about this issue with him. Though, as our respective lives get busier, there is a growing distance between ourselves and our families."*

Now it's your turn. Be introspective, be factual, and consider the situation from their perspective. Do not vilify your NSR.

What stands between you and that ideal NSR?

____

____

____

____

Both questions provide excellent opportunities to engage with your NSR and uncover any blind spots in your thinking.

However, if your relationship is not yet ready for such discussions, congratulate yourself for engaging in self-reflection, as you are taking the first step toward personal improvement and growth.

As the Chinese philosopher Lao Tzu famously said, "The journey of a thousand miles begins with a single step." By starting this book and embarking on the journey of improving your NSR, you have already demonstrated leadership and initiative. Regardless of who ultimately joins you on this adventure, you will grow and evolve through the experience.

Working on your NSR can be one of the most challenging and rewarding investments you make, though if you remember that the goal is not perfection, but progress, you will invariably achieve it.

Chapter Takeaways

- Begin by understanding your current starting point and the desired direction for your relationship.
- Recognize perfect relationships don't exist, and the journey toward improvement is ongoing.
- Improving involves envisioning the ideal and identifying the obstacles that may impede progress.

Exercise

For this week, much of the exercise was completed within the chapter. As such, the only "homework" is to gut-check your thinking by asking your NSR about their ideal relationship.

If the relationship is in a relatively good place today and you scored above 22 on your Relationship Assessment Scale, consider inviting your NSR to also engage in the exercises. Conversely, *if the relationship is seriously challenged and stressed, asking them to engage this way may be premature.* It may not be welcome, and could even be ill-advised.

Use your judgment to determine how well it is likely to be received—if at all—and how well you can handle their response. There may be more work to be done in the chapters ahead before you can engage in constructive dialogue. Even in the best relationships, having a conversation with your NSR will require some measure of courage and vulnerability. Proceed at your comfort level, and we'll delve into the topics from these exercises in the chapters ahead.

If you did a gut check with your NSR, what insights emerged from that conversation?

How would your NSR characterize the primary challenges? (If you did not or cannot ask, take a guess at what they might say.)

How would your NSR characterize or describe the ideal relationship? (If you did not or cannot ask, take a guess at what they might say.)

Further Readings and Resources

- **"The relationship assessment scale."** Dicke, A., & Hendrick, C. (1998). *Journal of Social and Personal Relationships*, 15, 137–142.

- **"Reliability and validity of the relationship assessment scale."** Vaughn, M. J., & Baier, M. E. M. (1999). *American Journal of Family Therapy*, 27, 137–147.

- **Online sources** available in Appendix I.

chapter three

Tracking Progress

Progress is not in enhancing what is, but in advancing toward what will be.

—Khalil Gibran

HOW MANY TIMES have you bought the gym membership, got all the gear, and downloaded the music—only to lose motivation when you didn't turn into an Olympian in a week? Relationships are kind of like that. Improvement takes time, and it can be disheartening if you don't see results as quickly as you'd like. But here's the trick to staying engaged and committed to the process: start measuring. Yes, measure your relationship progress.

Why Track Relationship Progress?

Tracking progress might not sound intimate or romantic, but it works. Psychologists have observed the *mere-measuring effect*, which suggests that simply measuring something will increase the likelihood of success with it.[17] Just like logging your miles when you're training for a marathon (or let's be real, a 5K), tracking relationship progress helps you stay focused on improvement rather than perfection. I repeat: *our goal is not perfection, but improvement.* While we've identified our ideal, our focus should be on making progress toward it, not bringing every tiny detail into reality.

Conversely, failure to recognize small wins and track our progress can lead to discouragement. So when you measure the tiny steps forward, even if you take the occasional step back, you'll see how far you've come. And rest assured, it's worth it.

The Relationship Fitbit: Milestone Mapping and Satisfaction Ratings

So what's the relationship equivalent of a Fitbit? Enter Milestone Mapping and Satisfaction Ratings—your new go-to tools for tracking progress.

- ***Milestone Mapping:*** Identify specific behaviors, situations, or patterns you want to improve. It can be as simple as agreeing on a vacation without arguing (beach or mountains?) or working on a project together without tension or toxic behavior patterns. Each milestone you hit is a small victory, and the more milestones you conquer, the better your relationship becomes.

- ***Satisfaction Rating:*** Whether through self-assessments, journaling, or open conversations with your NSR, use simple questions like, "On a scale of 1 to 10, how satisfied are you/

am I in this relationship?" Even if the initial response is low due to relationship challenges, small improvements that raise the rating from a 2 to a 3 can provide motivation and a psychological boost and keep you moving forward.

But Doesn't Tracking Relationships Feel . . . Unnatural?

Some people think relationships should just "happen." No tracking. No effort. But that overlooks basic human psychology. Think about any big goal you've achieved—whether it's completing a degree, running a race, or saving up for something important. You celebrated milestones, didn't you? Relationships deserve the same kind of attention.

The more you incorporate Milestone Mapping and Satisfaction Rating into your relationship journey, the more motivated you become. You'll start to see that relationships are dynamic, always evolving. And by tracking your progress, you can enjoy the journey without feeling like you're stuck in neutral.

To help you along, starting with this chapter, each subsequent chapter will conclude with a satisfaction rating question, asking you, *"On a scale of 1 to 10 (with 10 being the most positive and 1 being the most negative), how satisfied are you with your North Star Relationship?"*

Whether this self-assessment occurs weekly or monthly,* the

---

* Research suggests that the more frequent the monitoring the more effective it is. Though, obviously, monitoring it hourly or even daily could be excessive. As such, we will align it with the completion of each chapter. This weekly cadence of self-assessments will be both convenient and powerful.

important thing is to write down the results and gain a sense of trajectory for the relationship over time.

The Four Stages of Progress (and How They Apply to Relationships)

Keep in mind that initially, tracking your progress requires some extra effort and focus, but with practice, it becomes second nature. Every new endeavor involves a learning curve where we move from unconscious incompetence to unconscious competence. The process looks something like this:

1. **Unconscious Incompetence:** You don't know what you don't know. You're blissfully unaware of what needs improving.

2. **Conscious Incompetence:** You realize what's wrong, and it's not fun. But now you're ready to work on it.

3. **Conscious Competence:** You've learned what to do, but it still takes effort. Like riding a bike with training wheels.

4. **Unconscious Competence:** Boom! You're in the zone. With dedicated practice and repetition, we've mastered a skill and it's second nature to us.

In relationships, you'll move through these stages too. At first, it might feel awkward to track progress, but over time, it feels more natural and may even give you a sense of mastery. That's when real transformation happens.

Important Caveat

While tracking progress can provide clarity and direction, relationships are dynamic and should not be reduced solely to metrics. Milestone Mapping and Satisfaction Ratings are tools meant to help you reflect and adjust, but they should never replace emotional connection, spontaneous moments, or authentic conversations. Experts like psychologist John Gottman emphasize that the heart of a healthy relationship lies in the everyday emotional exchanges between partners. Keep tracking light and don't let it overwhelm the natural flow of the relationship.

Chapter Takeaways

- **Track your progress to see improvements. Small wins build big results.**
- **Celebrate along the way. It's the journey, not the destination.**
- **Milestone Mapping and Satisfaction Ratings are great tools for your relationship growth.**

Exercise

Grab a pen and complete this sentence: "I would know our relationship is improving if . . ." Start small. Maybe it's about having a more peaceful meal together or just having a conversation without one of you rolling your eyes. Which milestones would go on your Milestone Map?

"I would know that our relationship is improving if . . . "

____

____

____

____

____

____

On a scale of 1 to 10 (with 10 being the most positive and 1 being the most negative), how satisfied are you with your North Star Relationship? __

Please answer this question on a weekly basis, or at whatever intervals you consume each chapter. This will allow you to track your progress.

To benefit from the analytics and data associated with the trajectory of your journey, please track your progress within your konnect better app or online at konnectbetter.com. The app will also allow you to set helpful reminders or prompts and maintain a dual tracker with your NSR.

Further Readings & Resources

- ***Atomic Habits,*** by James Clear
- ***The Progress Principle:*** *Using Small Wins to Ignite Joy, Engagement, and Creativity at Work*, by Teresa Amabile and Steven Kramer
- ***SuperBetter:*** *The Power of Living Gamefully*, by Jane McGonigal
- ***Switch:*** *How to Change Things When Change Is Hard*, by Chip Heath and Dan Heath
- **Online Source:** For additional Milestone Mapping ideas, tools, and templates, visit konnectbetter.com.

chapter four

Shared Purpose

He who has a why can endure any how.

—Friedrich Nietzsche

PICTURE TWO PEOPLE IN A ROWBOAT. They're both rowing hard, putting in all their effort, but they're facing opposite directions. No matter how strong or determined they are, they won't get very far. This is what happens in relationships when you're not aligned on a shared purpose. You may be working hard, but if you're not rowing toward the same goal, you're just going in circles.

Identifying a shared purpose ensures you're both rowing toward the same destination. It doesn't just make the journey smoother; it makes it possible to actually get somewhere together.

Why Shared Purpose Matters

Beloved French author Antoine de Saint-Exupéry once said, "If you want to build a ship, don't drum up people to gather wood.

Instead, teach them to yearn for the endless sea."* In other words, when you share a purpose, you're no longer just going through the motions. You're working together toward something bigger.

Throughout history, there are numerous examples of successful relationships that were united by a shared purpose. Consider the scientific powerhouse couple, Marie and Pierre Curie, who worked together to discover radium and polonium, earning them the Nobel Prize in physics. Or think of aviation pioneers like the Wright brothers, Wilbur and Orville, who built the first successful airplane.

While these examples involve extraordinary individuals, the significance of aligning on a shared purpose applies to all relationships. Research shows that couples and partners who know why they're together experience higher satisfaction, more bonding, and less conflict.[18] It's like having a GPS for your relationship. You still hit bumps in the road, but at least you know where you're going.

In many of our relationships, we often neglect to articulate their purpose.† Consequently, the relationship may feel more like an accommodation rather than a true partnership and collaboration. This leads to a focus on our differences; our attention flows toward what divides us rather than what unites us. Miscommunications and misunderstandings are addressed in isolation rather than within a broader context.

---

* Antoine de Saint-Exupéry was a French military war hero and acclaimed author. In addition, he is known for his role in persuading the Americans to enter the war against the Nazis. As a master in the art of persuasion, he knew that a compelling "why" can overcome any "how."

† Coming up with a "why" or shared purpose for the relationship with a romantic partner or with our children may be considerably harder than doing so for a business partner or an employee, but it is a worthy endeavor regardless.

How to Find Your Shared Why

Without an audacious purpose like discovering radium or inventing planes, how do we start defining our shared purpose? Here are a few things to consider.

- Reflect on your own why: Take a moment to think about what you want from this relationship. What are your values? What do you hope to achieve together?

- Communicate openly: Share your thoughts with your partner, and listen—really listen—to theirs. You might be surprised by what you learn.

- Create a shared vision: Can you articulate a common goal? Maybe it's something big, like starting a family, or something smaller, like being more present for each other. Whatever it is, write it down and use it as the beacon for your relationship.

When Things Get Tough, Remember Your Why

Even with a clear purpose, every relationship hits rough patches. That's when revisiting your "why" becomes even more important. Instead of focusing on the conflict, remind each other of the bigger picture. Next time you're in the middle of a heated debate, try saying something like:

> *"Hey, I know we're both upset right now, but can we agree that this relationship is worth finding a solution for because of (fill in shared purpose)?"*

*Pause. Get confirmation, as aligning with a shared purpose requires commitment from both parties.**

"If so, let's work together on this—because we both want it to succeed."

Trust me, it's harder to stay mad when you remember you're both on the same team.

Addressing the immediate emotions that are blocking progress often helps elevate the conversation and refocus on the shared purpose. Once that purpose is acknowledged, there will be greater commitment and creativity in finding a solution that aligns with everyone's goals. To quote the great conductor Benjamin Zander, "[We need to remember that] we are here to cross the swamp, not to fight with alligators."[19]

The Power of Reconnection

Think of your shared purpose as a reset button. Every time you lose sight of it, reconnecting can realign your relationship. You don't have to have grandiose goals. Sometimes the purpose of a relationship is just to be there for each other, to laugh, to cry, and to grow together.

Having clarity on the shared purpose continuously improves collaborative brainstorming to address both long-term aspirations and immediate concerns. The exercise itself of articulating

---

* This isn't always possible at every stage in the relationship. For example, a parent and a teenage child are unlikely to align on purpose. In this case, the teen does not have the maturity to be engaged in such an enlightened conversation, with only the parent being clear on the purpose, and they can communicate that to their teen.

that purpose, when done collaboratively, has the potential to rebuild and strengthen mutual commitment.

Chapter Takeaways

- A shared purpose gives your relationship direction and meaning.
- Aligning on purpose can help transcend daily conflicts.
- When things get tough, return to your shared why–it's your relationship's anchor.

Exercise

Take a few minutes to write down why your relationship matters. What are you both working toward? Is it a peaceful home? A strong friendship? Write it down, share it, and revisit it often. You may want to consider the "why" of your NSR, as spelled out in the "ideal" of chapter 2. Craft a relationship purpose statement that you can jointly agree to and commit to collaborate on together.

[**On a scale of 1 to 10, how satisfied are you with your North Star Relationship? __**]

Further Readings and Resources

- ***Start with Why,*** by Simon Sinek
- ***Find Your Why:*** *A Practical Guide for Discovering Purpose for You and Your Team*, by Simon Sinek, David Mead, and Peter Docker
- ***Conscious Loving:*** *The Journey to Co-Commitment*, by Gay Hendricks and Kathlyn Hendricks

chapter five

Expectations

Life is largely a matter of expectation.

—Horace

WHAT WOULD HAPPEN if you walked into a Michelin-starred restaurant expecting a gourmet meal, only to be served a soggy salad and overcooked chicken? That's what relationships can feel like when your expectations are out of sync with reality—disappointment on a plate.

Dale Carnegie once said, "Success is getting what you want. Happiness is wanting what you get." So happiness in relationships is inextricably linked with managing expectations. It's simple math: Happiness = Reality − Expectations.

The Expectation Trap

We live in a time where expectations are skyrocketing in every area of our lives. Take marriage, for example. Psychotherapist and author Esther Perel highlights that marriage used to serve the narrow purpose of survival and procreation. (Not the most romantic of reasons, but hey, it worked.) Over time, it has evolved to include various roles and responsibilities that spouses are expected to fulfill. Today, the expectations from marriage have become overwhelming.[20] We expect our partners to embody numerous qualities and fulfill multiple roles, from being an attractive lover to being a wise counselor, a capable coparent, a financial contributor, a problem solver, and even an identity shaper, all rolled into one. That's . . . a ludicrous lot.

This phenomenon extends beyond marriage. Parents, partners, and friends are also burdened by increasingly high expectations, while employers strive to meet employees' ever-growing demands for fulfillment and satisfaction in the workplace.

Is it any wonder that relationships struggle? We're asking one person to meet all our needs, and honestly, that's like trying to get one app to do everything on your phone. Spoiler alert: It's not going to happen, and when it doesn't, we feel let down.

Setting Realistic Expectations

Here's where we get into trouble: we expect too much, often without realizing it. And when those expectations don't line up with reality, we're left feeling disappointed, frustrated, or even resentful. Anne Lamott put it perfectly: "Expectations are resentments waiting to happen."

So how do we fix this? It starts with recognizing that no one person, relationship, or situation can fulfill every need. And that's okay. Instead of asking for perfection, we need to focus on what's realistic.

To effectively manage expectations, we must begin by clearly outlining what is healthy and realistic within our relationships. There are a handful of common examples of healthy and unhealthy expectations in the tables on the following pages. Simply by being more conscious of these examples and more modest with our expectations, we can find greater contentment in our relationships.

Unhealthy Expectations	Healthy Expectations
They are perfect and level-headed all the time.	They're imperfect, they will lose their cool, and they will say things to you that are disappointing, aggravating, and enraging.
They can read my mind and understand me.	They cannot read your mind, and patterns that are abundantly obvious to you are not obvious to them.
When I say __, they should pick up on that.	You likely communicate in different ways, and when you say "XYZ," they may hear "ABC." Understand the differences in how you communicate.
They will make me happy.	They will try to make you happy and fail because their job is not to make you happy but to be the best version of themselves.
They want what I want and enjoy similar interests.	They have very different needs, wants, interests, hobbies, and expectations than you do. This is worth exploring.
They can tend to all my emotional needs.	You both need multiple sources of emotional nourishment (e.g., friends, hobbies, passions, therapy, etc.).
They have nothing to be jealous of.	They will be jealous, fearful, and insecure. Those are normal feelings from people that don't always know what's in your head.
Everyone in my life will love them.	Not if they're human. Even the nicest, kindest people don't resonate with everyone. Be prepared for someone that you like to dislike them.

Unhealthy Expectations	Healthy Expectations
"I will fix them" or "They will fix me."	Not going to happen. Old wounds, blemishes, and traumas will surface. We can support each other through understanding and empathy, but the actual "fixing" must be done alone.
It should be easier than this.	Falling in love is easy; staying in love takes work. That work is hard.
There's a way for them to show me they love me.	There's your way, and there's their way. People show love in very different ways. Understand theirs and explain yours to them.
They will support everything I do.	Nope. There will be times when your values, principles, or decisions clash, and they will oppose what you're contemplating. That is perfectly healthy.
We tell each other everything.	Total transparency is nearly impossible and limits the privacy that every individual is entitled to have.
Everything in the relationship should be divided equally.	No relationship is equal all the time. Sometimes one gives more, spends more, bleeds more than the other. At other times it's reversed. Relationships must be fair, not equal.

The Social Media Effect

It doesn't help that social media is out here making everyone look perfect, with filtered lives and #relationshipgoals. We start comparing ourselves to those highlight reels and expect our lives to match others. Furthermore, the rapid pace of technology and access to information creates the illusion that everything, including our relationships, can be accelerated or adjusted to fit our desired timelines and outcomes.* But here's the truth: those manicured versions of people's lives aren't real. They're curated. Real life? It's messy, imperfect, and full of missteps, and it takes time to improve. Though that's exactly the space where real growth happens.

Finding the Balance

If we were to wrap up this chapter by saying, "Just lower your expectations," that would be incomplete (and a little depressing). We can't have zero expectations; we just need to adjust them to something more realistic. Also, lowering one's expectations should not be confused with lowering one's standards, which can lead to tolerating abuse or accepting bad behavior, which is neither healthy nor advisable. Instead, it is important to strike a balance between setting realistic expectations and maintaining our dignity. This includes expecting kindness, respect, and mutual support from the people you love. Low expectations aren't the goal. Healthy, realistic ones are.

---

* The irony of this book being an expedited path of improving relationships is not lost on us. The phenomenon is true, notwithstanding that we are attempting to leverage it.

Important Caveat

While setting realistic expectations is key to avoiding disappointment, it's also important to acknowledge that unmet expectations can offer opportunities for growth. Conflict and disappointment are natural parts of relationships and provide the chance to deepen intimacy through vulnerability. Relationships are about more than just getting what you want. They're about learning and growing together, even in the face of imperfection.

Chapter Takeaways

- Expectations are on the rise in our modern relationships, but so is dissatisfaction.
- Setting realistic expectations is about finding balance, not lowering standards.
- Healthy expectations strengthen relationships, while unrealistic ones weaken them.

Exercise

Notice which unhealthy expectations you carry. (If you get stuck, consider using the referenced examples within the chapter as a starting point.) At a minimum, pick one expectation you've been holding on to that's been causing frustration. Ask yourself: Is it realistic? How can you adjust it? And don't forget to communicate it—because mind reading isn't part of the deal.

Stop during any frustrating moment and take stock of which expectation is going unmet.

What expectations were unmet? *(Feel free to focus purely on the emotions here without judgment or concern for rationality.)*	
Were these expectations reasonable and healthy? *(Feel free to apply judgment here, taking a slightly more rational approach.)*	
How might we right-size the expectations for the future? *(NSR collaboration here is preferred as part of this reconciliation process.)*	

On a scale of 1 to 10, how satisfied are you with your North Star Relationship? __

Further Readings and Resources

- ***The All-or-Nothing Marriage:*** *How the Best Marriages Work,* by Eli J. Finkel

- **"Should spouses be demanding less from marriage?** A contextual perspective on the implications of interpersonal standards," McNulty, J. K. (2016). *Personality and Social Psychology Bulletin,* 42, 444–457.

chapter six

The Nuances of Trust

To be trusted is a greater compliment than being loved.

—George MacDonald

IMAGINE THAT YOU ARE A SENIOR OFFICER in an elite unit of the military. You are reviewing an incoming crop of candidates. Your choices will have life-and-death implications for both soldiers and civilians, so what characteristics are you prioritizing—strength, speed, intelligence, creativity, endurance?

According to Simon Sinek, the navy's elite unit, Navy SEAL Team 6, prioritizes individuals with a strong capacity for trust over those who achieve higher performance.[21] The navy understands that exceptionalism in certain traits cannot compensate for the absence of impeccable trust, which is crucial for navigating life's challenging journeys.

What Exactly Is Trust?

It's almost cliché to say that trust is vital to every relationship, acting as both the lubricant and the foundation. With mutual trust, any challenge can be overcome, while even minor issues can be magnified when trust is lacking. If the Navy SEALs are choosing trust over talent, that's a strong signal of its importance. But before we talk about how to increase trust, we should at least make sure we know what we're talking about. So what exactly is trust?

Having raised several teenagers of my own, I can vouch that it's nearly impossible to bring a teenager into adulthood without hearing some variation of the phrase, "I can't believe you don't trust me!" And unfortunately, most parents (like yours truly) find themselves unprepared for such assertions. That's largely because the way we talk about trust is too simplistic.

To engage in a meaningful discussion on trust with our loved ones, we must distinguish between the various forms of trust, clearly understanding which aspects of trust are present or absent in each relationship. Studies suggests that trust encompasses three overarching components: *character*, *competence*, and *comfort*.[22]

Character: The Root of Trust

Character is the foundation. It's the integrity and intent behind a person's actions. When someone's character is solid, you trust them to do the right thing—even when it's hard.

- **Integrity:** Do they live what they preach? Are they honest, even when it's tough? Trust in someone's integrity is what lets you hand them the keys to your life (or your car).

- **Intent:** Why are they doing what they're doing? Do they have your best interests at heart, or are they just looking out for themselves? You can only trust someone if you believe they're in it for the right reasons, which can be compromised if we suspect their intentions to be contrary to our interests.*

Competence: Can They Follow Through?

Character is great, but it's not enough. If you trust someone's heart but not their ability to get the job done, trust falls apart.

- **Capability:** Do they have the skills, judgment, and knowledge to handle what's important to you? Trust is knowing they can not just show up but also show up ready to perform.

---

* Naturally, behavior is often the closest indication of intent we have. ("If you say you care, why don't you act like it?") When there's a breakdown in trust, it may be a function of behavior disconnected from intent. That requires simple realignment through good communication.

- **Reliability:** Do they keep their promises, and do they reliably manage their commitments? You can't build trust with someone who often flakes out at the last minute.

Comfort: Can You Be Yourself?

Even if someone has good character and competence, there's one last piece: comfort. Do you feel safe and understood with them?

- **Understanding:** Do they really get you—your values, your dreams, your quirks? When someone truly understands who you are, trust flourishes.

- **Safety:** Can you be vulnerable with them? Trust is being able to share your weirdest thoughts, your deepest fears, or your biggest dreams without worrying about how they'll react.

Taking a more nuanced approach to trust allows us to recognize that trust can be compromised when any aspect of it is stressed. It's also possible for someone to do all the right things but in the wrong way or fail to communicate and meet expectations. The main takeaway is that trust is like a three-legged stool: you've got character, competence, and comfort. Take one leg away, and the whole thing wobbles—or worse, you're splayed out on the floor, wondering what just happened.

Rebuilding When Trust Breaks

Trust isn't bulletproof. It gets chipped away by misunderstandings, unmet expectations, or miscommunication. But here's the thing: trust can be rebuilt. Start by figuring out where it broke. Was it character, competence, or comfort? Once you know where the crack is, you can work together to fix it.

Being Trusted Involves Being Trusting

It's important to note that both parties have a role to play in a trusting relationship. Trust is the combination of being both trusting and trustworthy—the ability to trust others and be trusted by them. While we have a responsibility to be trustworthy, it is also essential to be trusting.

Today, trust is often secured with structures, contracts, and constitutions, rather than our collective goodwill. Just consider what's involved in any partnership, employment, or even marriage. And while these structures are necessary, they prioritize prevention rather than connection. Emphasizing rules, policies, and protective measures focuses more on deterrence, instead of proactively building trust. Yet our intimate relationships can only be secured through trust in one's character, competence, and comfort.

Chapter Takeaways

- Trust is multifaceted, with three key elements: character, competence, and comfort.
- If trust is broken, first identify where—then focus on rebuilding that piece.
- Both being trustworthy and being trusting are keys to fostering a healthy relationship.

Exercise

Think about your most important relationship. Where is trust the strongest? And where is it wobbly? If appropriate, talk with your NSR about these aspects and ask where they think you could improve. And if the circumstances of the relationship won't allow you to ask them, reflect on what they've said to you in the past and how they may answer the question.

Aspects of Trust*	Reflect on where—either by my own recognition or the recognition of my NSR—there may be most potential for improvement.	What might a small improvement here look like?
Integrity: Where might I compromise my honesty, consistency, or values?		
Intent: Where might my motives or interests be misaligned with my NSRs?		

---

* Please bear in mind that many of these are intertwined, so you won't necessarily find an example or response for each aspect, and there may be some natural intersections or overlap. The questions are merely intended to prompt new insights and expand your thinking.

Aspects of Trust	Reflect on where—either by my own recognition or the recognition of my NSR—there may be most potential for improvement.	What might a small improvement here look like?
Capability: Where might I have gaps in my skills, capacities, or knowledge?		
Reliability: Where have I failed to live up to my commitments?		
Understanding: Where have I misunderstood the concerns, needs, or aspirations of my NSR?		
Safety: Where have I made it difficult for my NSR to be open, vulnerable, and secure with me?		

On a scale of 1 to 10, how satisfied are you with your North Star Relationship? __

Further Readings and Resources

- ***Building Trust in Business, Politics, Relationships, and Life,*** by Robert C. Solomon and Fernando Flores
- ***I Love You, but I Don't Trust You:*** *The Complete Guide to Restoring Trust in Your Relationship*, by Mira Kirshenbaum
- ***The Courage to Trust,*** by Cynthia Lynn Wall

section two

ACTION

The Redemption of Caroline Cox

Caroline Cox had always prided herself on being the rational, measured sibling. She was the one who sought compromise when Alex's ego clashed with Helena's defiance. But when the buyout occurred, and she was effectively cast out of the business her grandfather built, she was consumed by anger. The betrayal festered, and for months she found herself slipping into an abyss of bitterness. Every family gathering was a land mine, every conversation a reminder of her failure to hold the family together.

Then came the breaking point. A heated argument with her husband, Jeremy, ended with him saying, "You talk about Alex's arrogance, but you have the same blind spots. You never *ask* for what you want. You expect people to read your mind, and when they don't, you blame them."

The words landed like a gut punch. In that moment, Caroline saw herself clearly for the first time—not as a victim, but as a participant in the breakdown. If she had better understood her own emotions, if she had communicated her needs instead of assuming others should intuit them, could things have been different?

So she set out to rebuild—not her business empire, but herself. She devoured books on emotional intelligence, attended workshops on conflict resolution, and enlisted a coach to help her refine her ability to make clear, intentional requests. Instead of waiting for people to disappoint her, she articulated expectations. Instead of blaming, she took ownership. Slowly, she became someone who wasn't just reactive to the world around her but proactive in shaping it.

The transformation rippled through her life. Her marriage, once burdened by unspoken resentments, deepened into something far more resilient. Her children, now grown, began confiding in her in ways they never had before. And most surprisingly, she reconnected with Helena. They had been bound by their shared disdain for Alex, but now they bonded over something more profound: growth.

A decade after the Cox Industries debacle, Caroline found herself in an unexpected place—a boardroom. Not of a family empire, but leading a nonprofit she started and funded, focused on helping women develop leadership skills. She was thriving, not because she had reclaimed a throne, but because she had finally built the internal foundation to sustain real, meaningful relationships. She had learned to make better requests, own her decisions, and change her own patterns before expecting the world to change for her.

Then, one day, an invitation arrived in the mail. It was from Alex's oldest son, Nick. A wedding. Caroline hesitated before opening it, half expecting it to be another last-minute slight. But there, in Nick's own handwriting, were the words: "Our daughter, Lisa, is getting married this summer. We would love for you to be there. Let's start over."

Tears welled in her eyes. She had spent years mastering the art of communication, of understanding emotions—now, at last, it was paying off in the way that mattered most.

chapter seven

Emotional Fluency

Emotions are not problems to be solved. They are signals to be interpreted.

—Vironika Tugaleva

ONE NIGHT, my wife opened up to me, saying, "I'm feeling overwhelmed with everything going on and don't know how to keep up." Without thinking, I shot back, "Yup, you really have to manage your time better." Brilliant, right? If that wasn't emotionally tone-deaf enough, I once had an employee confide in me, "I've been feeling really unmotivated lately and struggling to stay focused on my projects." My response? "We just have to stay focused and push through."

Either of them could have given me a trophy for "Most Dismissive Response Ever." I skipped right past their emotional state and went straight into problem-solving mode—no empathy, no curiosity, just a focus on output over feelings. Unsurprisingly, the chilly responses I got in return were my wake-up calls to the critically important world of emotional fluency—the ability to hear beyond the words, respond with emotional awareness, and connect on a deeper level. Emotional fluency is what allows us to bypass the surface-level fluff and engage in meaningful, human conversations.

Emotions Aren't Just Background Noise

Let's talk about emotions for a second. Think of them like traffic lights. Green means "Go for it," red means "Stop in your tracks," and yellow? Well, that's your ambiguous "Proceed with caution" zone. Most of us are flying through emotional intersections without even noticing the lights. We're either running red lights or slamming on the brakes at green ones.

Emotional fluency is about learning to see those signals—both in ourselves and in others—and figuring out when it's time to push the gas or hit the brakes. At its core, emotional fluency is the art of understanding, interpreting, and responding to emotional cues with genuine curiosity. Because here's the thing: emotions aren't random background noise. They're data, telling us something important. But you can't interpret the signals if you're not paying attention.

Skip the Small Talk: Get Real

Want to have a real conversation that means something? Here's a tip: ditch the "How are you?" and upgrade to "What's top of mind these days?" Trust me, it works like magic. Instead of the generic "I'm fine" or "Not much," you'll get real responses like:

> *"Thanks for asking. I'm stressed about work. My business is struggling, and I'm not sure how to fix it."*

"Honestly? I'm exhausted. My kid's been sick, and nothing seems to be working."

"I'm thinking about proposing, and I'm freaking out a little. Is that normal?"

Boom. Now you're in. The most powerful emotions dictate what we think about. So when you ask people what's on their minds, you're not just getting the "I'm fine" surface-level stuff—you're getting to the good stuff.

This is emotional fluency in action. It's the ability to communicate on a deeper level, to tune into the emotions that are bubbling beneath the surface. And the best part? Once you start tuning in, the connection becomes real. You're building trust, creating safety, and making space for genuine attachment.

Emotional Connections Are Built on Feelings, Not Facts

Let's face it: most of us try to navigate relationships with logic. We think if we just explain ourselves clearly enough, everything will work out. Spoiler alert: It won't. Relationships aren't built on facts; they're built on feelings. Sure, you need some rationality to keep things balanced, but the real glue that holds us together? Emotions.

Superficial or transactional relationships don't require this depth, but if you want to move past the surface and build something meaningful, emotional fluency is your new best friend. It's about being able to connect with someone's feelings, not just their words.

Emotional Fluency Starts with You

Here's the kicker: you can't get good at tuning into other people's emotions if you're clueless about your own. It's like trying to speak a language without knowing the alphabet. If you want to connect deeply, you need to start with yourself.

How do we do that?

Thinkers as early as Aristotle believed in the notion of core emotions or primary families of emotions. In contemporary times, this idea was most effectively expressed through the wheel of emotions, as illustrated on the next page. The wheel of emotions was developed by psychologist Robert Plutchik, as a visual representation of primary emotions, helping people put a name to specific emotions, considering their varying nuances and complexities, and helping individuals develop greater self-awareness. The wheel outlines the basic emotions, sometimes signified by varying colors and relating to the central emotion in the middle. For example, for the emotion "anger," the lesser degree is annoyance, represented on the outer edge of the slice, and the greater degree is rage, situated by the center of the emotion wheel. (In Plutchik's depiction, the sections are arranged in a flower shape with each "petal" representing one emotion.*)

Can't figure out what you're feeling? Give it a spin. Are you angry? Anxious? Excited? Sometimes it's hard to name what's going on inside, but when you do, everything clicks into place. And the better you get at recognizing your own emotions, the better you'll be at sensing what other people are feeling.

---

* A more elaborate range of emotions was developed by educator Tom Drummond and can be accessed here: https://www.simonwhatley.co.uk/content/writing/vocabulary-of-emotions/vocabulary-of-emotions.pdf.

Whether it's our own emotions or those of others, simply acknowledging them can provide a sense of comfort. For example, when a child cries, a parent might say, "I sense that you're feeling sad, ashamed, and abandoned. Is that right?" If the child confirms, they will immediately feel understood and experience some relief from their pain. Even if we guess incorrectly, empathy is often appreciated. The child may correct us, but this opens the door to a meaningful conversation.

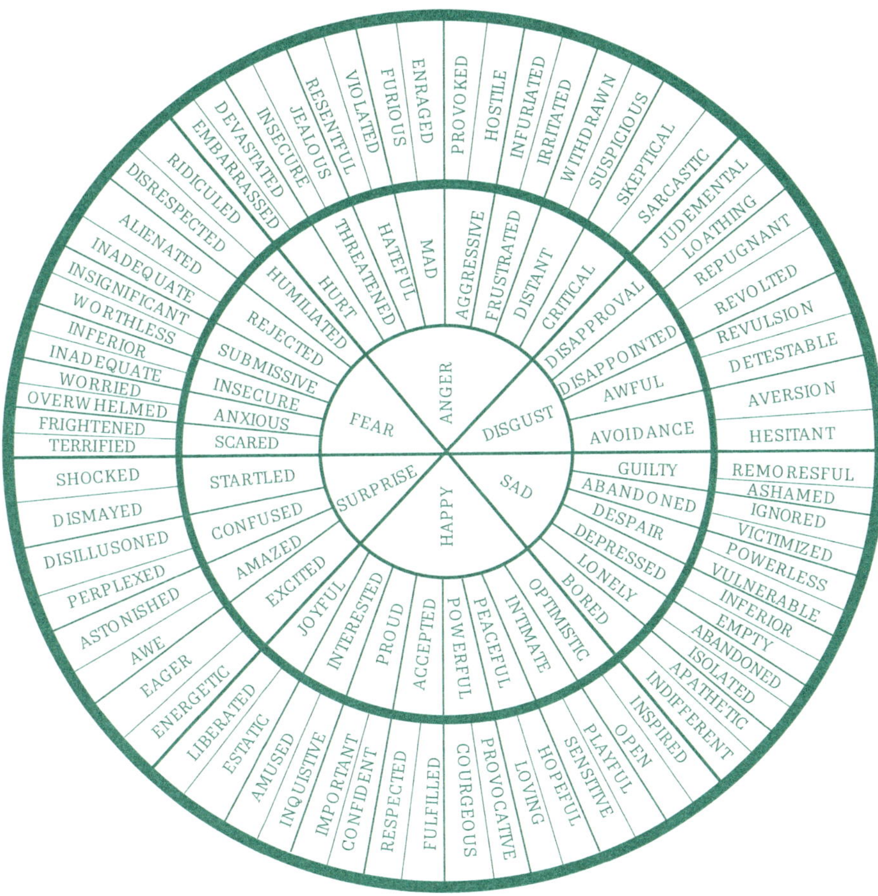

Express, Don't Attack

Let's clear something up: expressing your emotions isn't an excuse to attack someone. Saying, "I feel like you're being a jerk" is not emotional fluency. That's just throwing shade, and nobody's going to respond well to that.

Instead, stick to the real feelings. Say, "I feel hurt" or "I'm frustrated." See the difference? It's not about "you" but just an admission of my feelings. One opens the door to connection, and the other slams it shut. To be more specific . . .

Don't say: "I feel like you tried to hurt me."

Do say: "I feel hurt and upset."

Accusations make people defensive, but real emotions invite empathy. The moment someone understands that you're genuinely expressing how you feel—not attacking them—they're far more likely to respond with kindness instead of defensiveness.

From Small Talk to Deep Connections

If you take only thing from this chapter, we hope it will be the simple recognition that what people say to you is far less important than how they say it. And building relationships requires us to tell the difference.

Picture this: you come home from a long day, and your partner looks upset. Or you walk into your kid's room and see them scowling. You ask, "What's wrong?" They say, "Nothing." You know that's not true, but now what? Here's where emotional fluency comes in. Instead of brushing it off, you might say, "You seem upset. I just want to make sure you know I'm here for you if you want to talk."

That's emotional fluency in action: reading the signs, acknowledging the feelings, and making room for a deeper connection.

Chapter Takeaways

- Emotional fluency is the ability to tune into your own emotions and those of others, creating deeper, more meaningful connections.
- To be emotionally fluent, you have to start with yourself. Learn to recognize and name your feelings before you can understand someone else's.
- Emotions are for sharing, not for weaponizing or attacking. Speak your truth without passing blame.

Exercise

This week, check in with yourself a few times. When you feel something—whether it's stress, joy, anger, or confusion—take a moment to name it. Use the wheel of emotions if you need to. Then try tuning in to the emotions of the people around you. What are they feeling? What signals are they giving you? Jot it down. Practice the language of emotions, as practice makes fluency, and see how your conversations deepen.

Prompt	Mood	Emotions

[On a scale of 1 to 10, how satisfied are you with your North Star Relationship? __]

Further Readings and Resources

- ***Emotional Intelligence:*** *Why It Can Matter More Than IQ*, by Daniel Goleman

chapter eight

Secondary Emotions

Every time you are tempted to react in the same old way, ask if you want to be a prisoner of the past or a pioneer of the future.

—Deepak Chopra

THINK ABOUT THAT MOMENT when someone sharply cuts you off in traffic. Your first instinct is fear—your heart skips a beat, your hands tighten on the wheel. But then, in a matter of seconds, that fear transforms into pure fury, and suddenly you're imagining all kinds of creative ways to let them know just how reckless they are. This is the classic example of secondary emotions.

The first wave of fear was your primary emotion, a natural reaction to the situation. But that rage? That's the secondary emotion creeping in, distorting things, and turning a simple moment of fear into something much bigger. And we've all been there.

The Buddha and the Two Arrows

There's an old Buddhist parable where the Buddha asks his student, "If you're hit by an arrow, is it painful?" The student nods—obviously, getting hit by an arrow hurts. Then the Buddha asks, "And if you're hit by a second arrow, does it hurt even more?" Again, the student nods, albeit more hesitantly, wondering where this is going.

The Buddha then explains that while both are painful, there's a profound difference between the two. With the first arrow, it might have been out of our control. Life can sometimes throw us a curveball or an arrow. However, allowing the second arrow to hit? That's on us. We could have reacted and changed our positioning after having been hit by the first arrow. Yet we allowed ourselves to stay in the line of fire.

There's hardly a better analogy than Buddha's second arrow to explain secondary emotions. Distinguishing between primary and secondary emotions is central to our general understanding of emotions.

Primary versus Secondary Emotions: What's the Difference?

Secondary emotions are like that second arrow. We can't always stop the first blow—the hurt, the fear, the embarrassment. But we do have a choice in how we handle what comes next. To be more specific . . .

- **Primary emotions** are your gut reactions to an event. They're immediate and intense but tend to fade quickly.

- **Secondary emotions** are your responses to those primary emotions. They stick around longer, get more complicated, and often lead to actions you might regret.

Secondary emotions have the potential to wreck our relationships. They can lead us to react impulsively and engage in actions that we later regret. As Ambrose Bierce once said, "Speak when you are angry, and you will make the best speech you will ever regret."

Why Secondary Emotions Can Be Toxic

Here's the thing: secondary emotions can be sneaky. They often mask what's really going on underneath, making it harder to resolve conflicts or express what we're truly feeling. Instead of saying "I'm scared" or "I'm hurt," we lash out with anger or resentment. And while anger might feel powerful in the moment, it usually does more harm than good.

Let's go back to the driver who cut you off in traffic and nearly caused an accident. If the fury of that secondary emotion leads you to flip the bird without pausing to register who that other driver is, you might find yourself staring at your most valuable client (or now past client), your church pastor, or your mother's best friend.

Similarly, if someone humiliates you in front of a crowd, your primary emotion is embarrassment and shame. But then, almost immediately, that shame turns into anger. And that anger can stick around for days, fueling arguments, grudges, and passive-aggressive comments.

If you think about it, I'm sure you can recall a time when you snapped at someone over something small, only to realize later it wasn't really about them at all. Maybe your child made a snide comment to you earlier in the day, or maybe you were stressed about something completely unrelated. But your secondary emotions took over, and now you're in damage control mode with someone who didn't even see it coming.

How to Avoid the Second Arrow

Here's the good news: we can learn to dodge that second arrow. The first step is recognizing when a secondary emotion is taking over. When you feel that surge of anger or frustration, ask yourself: What am I really feeling? What's the primary emotion underneath all of this?

By comprehending the primary emotion, we can better cope with, respond to, and even avoid impulsive and accusatory reactions to secondary emotions, which may harm our relationships.* For example, instead of saying, "I'm livid that you didn't get this done," try saying, "I'm scared that if this doesn't get done, we'll be in trouble." Instead of saying, "I'm furious that you ignored me," try, "I'm hurt that my needs weren't heard."

By focusing on the primary emotion, you're opening the door to connection instead of conflict. You're showing vulnerability, which encourages empathy from the other person.

* Sometimes the most destructive secondary emotions we feel are those toward ourselves (e.g., feeling numb and cold because we are ashamed of something we've done, not having dealt with the primary emotions).

Chapter Takeaways

- Primary emotions are your initial, gut reactions. Secondary emotions are the lingering, more complex reactions that follow.
- Secondary emotions can often mask the real issue, making it harder to resolve conflicts.
- Recognizing and expressing primary emotions can prevent secondary emotions from taking over and damaging your relationships.

Exercise

To test your understanding, take a short quiz differentiating between primary and secondary emotions below. Answers to the quiz can be found after Further Readings and Resources at the very end of this chapter (but no cheating!).

Which type of emotion is being experienced here?

1. A direct reaction to an external event? ___________
2. It becomes more intense over time? ___________
3. Experienced more frequently than the events that prompted the emotion? ___________
4. Recedes over time as the event recedes? ___________
5. Interferes with existing relationships in the present and the future? ___________

6. Is the very first thing that you feel? __________

7. Is complex, ambiguous, and difficult to understand? __________

For a bit more introspection, and some practical exercises, consider which (if any) secondary emotions may be holding your relationship back. Think about where you might have exhibited anger, resentment, or frustration with your NSR.

____

____

____

____

Consider the root causes or primary emotions that may have triggered those secondary emotions.

____

____

____

____

Consider how you might address this with your NSR going forward.

____

____

____

____

On a scale of 1 to 10, how satisfied are you with your North Star Relationship? __

Further Readings and Resources

- ***The Language of Emotions:*** *What Your Feelings Are Trying to Tell You*, by Karla McLaren
- ***Nonviolent Communication:*** *A Language of Life*, by Marshall B. Rosenberg
- **"The 6 Types of Basic Emotions and Their Effect on Human Behavior,"** by Kendra Cherry. July 14, 2024: www.verywellmind.com/primary-emotions-2797378

Quiz Answers

1. Primary
2. Secondary
3. Secondary
4. Primary
5. Secondary
6. Primary
7. Secondary

chapter nine

Mastering Requests

You can have everything in life you want if you will just help enough other people get what they want.

—Zig Ziglar

OCCASIONALLY YOU'LL ASK SOMEONE to do something for you, and your request just . . . flops. Maybe you barked out a command, and they dug in their heels. Or maybe you made a vague request, and it never got done. In either case, you're left frustrated, and they're left feeling a little resentful. If you can relate, this chapter may help.

What we've all discovered (often the hard way) is that making requests isn't just about getting stuff done. It's about building bridges, not burning them. The way we ask for something can make all the difference in how people respond, whether they do it willingly—or do it while grumbling under their breath.

The Power of a Well-Placed Request

Take a cue from Franklin Delano Roosevelt. The story is told that Roosevelt once encountered a key senator who was blocking his legislation. Instead of engaging in a fight or argument, Roosevelt took a different approach. He discovered that the senator, like himself, was an avid stamp collector. Roosevelt invited the senator to his home and asked for his advice on stamp collecting. The senator, flattered by the request, eagerly came over that evening, and they spent time reviewing their collections together. No discussion about legislation took place. However, the next morning, when the bill came up for a vote, the senator voted with Roosevelt.

Although in this case, no formal request was made, the president used his powers of persuasion and connection to fortify the relationship, making an implicit request. And his investment paid off.

Stop Commanding, Start Requesting

Here's the thing: most of us, when we really want something, tend to go for the command. "Do this!" "Handle that!" But unless you're running a military drill, commands are more likely to backfire. No one enjoys being bossed around, especially by someone they're close to. When you issue a command, you strip people of their autonomy—and you might be surprised at how fast they push back.

This is especially relevant in a family business setting, where family members may report to us, blurring the lines between professional and familial roles.

So how do you make a request that people actually want to fulfill?

Here's a formula that has proven to be most effective for me:

1. **Give them the freedom to say no.** Phrases like "Would you be open to . . . " or "Could you help me with . . . " make it clear that they have a choice. And while leaders often hate hearing "no," the freedom to decline can make a "yes" feel so much more genuine.

2. **Embrace vulnerability.** Asking for help can feel uncomfortable, like you're admitting you need someone. Guess what? That's exactly the point. Vulnerability builds trust. You're not demanding; you're inviting collaboration.

3. **Communicate the why.** We often skip this part, assuming people just know why something is important. In reality, they may not. Explaining the context helps others understand why the task matters, and suddenly, they're more invested.

4. **Recognize their skills.** No one likes a blanket request that could be tossed at anyone. Tailor your ask: "I really value your expertise in . . . " or "This plays to your strengths in . . . " People love feeling seen and appreciated for what they bring to the table.

5. **Confirm commitment.** Don't just ask and assume they're all in. Make sure they have the bandwidth: "Do you have the time for this?" or "Is this something you feel you can commit to right now?" If they say yes, you're both on the same page.

6. **Offer support.** You don't have to go full-on superhero. Offer to help where you can: "Is there anything I can do to make this easier for you?" or "How can I assist you with this?" It shows that you're in it together.

A Yes Is Better When It's Genuine

Sometimes, a request gets a half-hearted "yes"—and honestly, that can be worse than a straight-up "no." You might get the task done, but the enthusiasm won't be there. That's why it's crucial to leave the door open for someone to say no. It's uncomfortable, sure, but it shows respect. If you really need their help, you can say, "If I have no other alternatives, I may need to come back to you. But I'll try to find other solutions first." This way, if they say "yes" later, it's because they genuinely want to help, not because they felt cornered.

From Request to Offer: Making It Even More Appealing

Here's a twist: What if, instead of asking for help, you made it feel like an opportunity? If you can frame your request as something that benefits them, you're more likely to get enthusiastic buy-in. This works especially well when the request aligns with their personal growth or interests. People are far more willing to say "yes" when they see how it benefits them.

Think of it as the difference between asking, "Can you do this for me?" and saying, "This is a great opportunity for you to showcase your skills / step up in your role / get noticed for your leadership." The second version isn't just a request—it's an offer they can't refuse.

Avoiding Resentment: A Playbook for Requests

To avoid clashes and resentment, it is our responsibility to provide additional context and clarity. Examples of this include:

- *To avoid personal resentment*: "Don't hesitate to say no to this request, but please do share your rationale with me."
- *In response to an accommodation*: "I'd rather not do this, but because I want to help you and value our relationship, I'm willing to step up here . . . "
- *Following a disappointing response made*: "I wish I could do this for you, but I cannot for the following reasons . . . "
- *Following a disappointing response received*: "If you can't do this, can I trouble you to let me know what you could do?"

It's Not Just *How* We Request, but Also *the Nature* of the Request

John Gottman promotes the utilization of his bagel compromise method, which emphasizes the importance of clearly delineating the areas in which individuals are open to compromise and those in which they are firm and unwilling to negotiate.[23]

In the bagel on the following page, the outer circle represents the flexible area in relationships where compromise is possible. The inner circle of the bagel represents our core values or fundamental needs on which people are rarely willing to compromise.

We can often mitigate conflict with our NSR simply by asking them explicitly about what may be within the confines of the outer layer versus the outer circle, and being clear on where each party needs to bend or adjust.

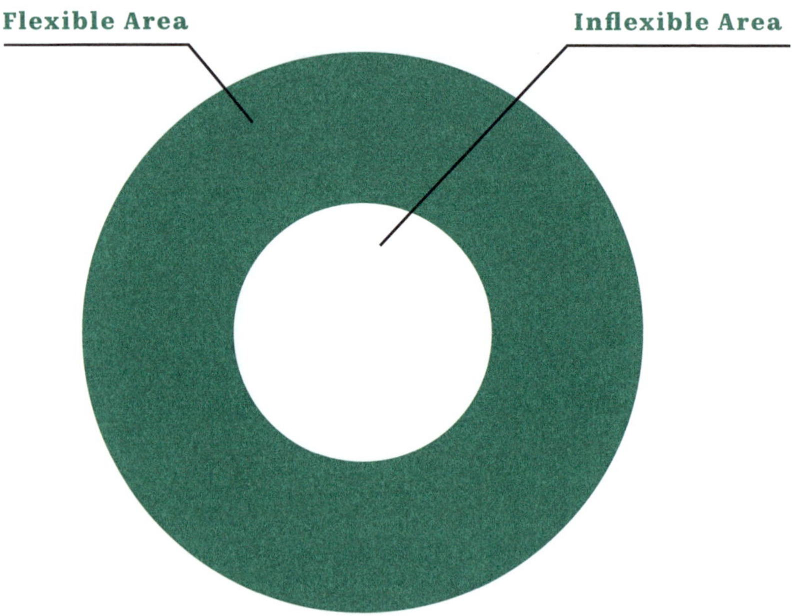

Mastering the Art of Negotiation

When you have a strong relationship, negotiation becomes easier. You can suggest, request, or demand—but remember, requests strike the perfect balance. Demands might get immediate results but at the cost of long-term goodwill, while suggestions can feel too weak. A well-placed request is both respectful and strong, showing that you value the other person's autonomy and trust their ability to make a choice.

Chapter Takeaways

- Mastering requests means giving people the space to say no, explaining the why, and offering support.
- Framing requests as opportunities, rather than demands, generates more enthusiasm and engagement.
- Clear requests require clear accountability, including deliverables, timelines, and metrics for success.

Exercise

Use the checklist below to practice making thoughtful requests:

	Request #1	Request #2	Request #3	Request #4
Can they say no? And how?				
Do they understand the why?				
Do they feel complimented and supported?				

	Request #1 ________ ________ ________	Request #2 ________ ________ ________	Request #3 ________ ________ ________	Request #4 ________ ________ ________
Did you confirm their commitment?				
Can the request be framed as an offer or advice?				
How will you assess it?				

[**On a scale of 1 to 10, how satisfied are you with your North Star Relationship? __**]

Further Readings and Resources

- ***The Power of Ask:*** *Ask for What You Want, Get What You Want,* by James Altucher and Claudia Azula Altucher
- ***The Art of Asking:*** *How I Learned to Stop Worrying and Let People Help*, by Amanda Palmer
- ***Ask!*** *The Bridge from Your Dreams to Your Destiny*, by Mark Victor Hansen and Crystal Dwyer Hansen

chapter ten

Decision Ownership

Cooperation is the thorough conviction that nobody can get there unless everybody gets there.

—Virginia Burden

YOU'RE AT A FAMILY DINNER, and the conversation turns to who made the decision to cancel last year's holiday gathering. Your aunt chimes in, saying, "Well, I wasn't even asked!" Your brother adds, "If I had known, I could've fixed everything!" Meanwhile, you're sitting there, knowing full well that you made the call because nobody else wanted to step up. And now? Somehow, it's all your fault.

In relationships, whether they're among family, work colleagues, or friends, when things look daunting or complex, few will take the lead, though with the benefit of hindsight, once situations look clearer in retrospect, everyone wants a say. Often, one person will make those complicated decisions on behalf of others. The matriarch may decide on the family's real estate, a father may decide which church the family belongs to, the sister may make business decisions for her disengaged brother, and Cousin Susie may always plan the annual family reunion. Though when things don't go as planned, everyone suddenly becomes an expert on what should've been done (e.g., "Why didn't you consult me?" or "I knew this wasn't going to work").

Mastering decision ownership, however, isn't about avoiding blame or keeping everyone happy. It's about clarity. It's about knowing who decides what, when, and how to make sure decisions actually stick.

The Dunning-Kruger Effect in Families

A pair of Cornell University psychologists, David Dunning and Justin Kruger, discovered what is today known as the Dunning-Kruger effect.[24] It states that those who don't know something are also less likely to recognize that they don't know something. In other words, people with low ability tend to overestimate their competence, while those with high competence may underestimate their abilities. Similarly, people who are least informed about a decision tend to be the most confident and vocal about how it *should* have been handled. It's like the family member who knows *nothing* about real estate but insists they could have gotten a better deal. Sound familiar?

The Solution? Define the Rules of the Game

If you want to minimize the friction and avoid every decision turning into a Monday morning quarterback session, you've got to establish some ground rules. Who gets a say, and when? Who makes the call on what? Here are four basic decision approaches:

- **Independent decisions:** Sometimes, it's your call. No discussion. End of story.
- **Consulted decisions:** Other times you'll solicit the input of others, but the final choice is still yours.
- **Voted decisions:** Everyone gets a vote, and majority rules.
- **Consensus decisions:** Everyone agrees before moving forward (good luck with that one).

The approach chosen depends on the type of decision, the stakes involved, and who might be affected by the decision. For minor, reversible decisions like choosing lunch or deciding on a route to work, independent choices are usually enough. However, for significant, irreversible decisions, such as selling a family home or changing careers, collaborating with and getting the input of those affected by the decision is essential. These decisions affect others and require alignment to ensure support and long-term success.

The Importance of Clarity

In business, we use tools like the RACI matrix (Responsible, Accountable, Consulted, and Informed) to sort out who does what. Why not bring some of that structure into your personal relationships? It's as simple as making sure everyone knows their role in the decision-making process.

For example, in my family, vacation planning is a consulted decision—my kids get input, but my wife and I make the final call. On the other hand, picking a restaurant is an independent decision because getting consensus with my kids is a pipe dream.

At the end of this chapter, you'll find a tool for using the RACI matrix in your own life and relationships.

When Your NSR Wants In on Every Decision

What happens when someone insists on being involved in decisions where their input isn't necessary? Everyone becomes incredibly frustrated, right? The trick is to understand *why* they want to be involved. Sometimes there's an underlying concern that needs to be addressed. Asking questions like, "What are you hoping to achieve by being involved?" can go a long way toward defusing tension and addressing their needs without adding unnecessary complexity.

Chapter Takeaways

- **Clear decision-making processes can prevent conflicts.**
- **Not every decision needs consensus. Sometimes independent calls are better. Consider each situation independently.**
- **When people insist on giving input, dig deeper to understand their concerns and prevent future conflicts.**

Exercise

Not all conflicts are rooted in decisions, but most decisions have the potential for conflict. Reflect on some of your recent decisions (or those of your NSR) that led to conflict. To help avoid friction with your NSR, consider how those decisions were made and how you think they could be changed for the better. Put a circle in the columns that mark how this type of decision is currently made and a check mark in the columns to indicate how it should be made. In the right-most column, explain your rationale.

After you've taken a stab at the chart below, have a conversation with your NSR about how to make the decision-making process smoother. Commit to one small tweak at a time.

Decision Types	Independent	Consulted	Voted	Consensus	Why?

On a scale of 1 to 10, how satisfied are you with your North Star Relationship? ___

Further Readings and Resources

- ***Wiser:*** *Getting Beyond Groupthink to Make Groups Smarter*, by Cass R. Sunstein and Reid Hastie

chapter eleven

Behavior Modification

You can't change the fruit without changing the root.

—Stephen R. Covey

WHEN MY ELDEST DAUGHTER was seven years old, she approached me with a sly grin and a riddle.

"Daddy, imagine there are five birds sitting on a wire, and three decide to fly away. How many are left?" Naturally, I applied my best dad math: "Two birds left, right?" She giggled and said, "No, Daddy, you'd still have five. Just because they *decided* to fly doesn't mean they actually *did*."

Bam. I'd just been schooled by a second grader on one of life's most important lessons: intentions alone don't count for much without action. And isn't that the truth in relationships? How many times have we thought, "I'm going to be better about showing appreciation" or "Next time, I'll really listen instead of just nodding along"? But thinking it and doing it are two very different things.

Words Are Easy, but Change Happens in Actions

Let's face it: saying that we'll change, promising we'll do better, and committing to working on a relationship can feel good. It can feel like progress just to say the words. But without changing our actual behavior, those promises are like birds that decide to fly away but never leave the wire. Relationships don't thrive on good intentions alone; they grow through action.

Action shapes mindset, not the other way around. You're not going to magically wake up with the perfect mindset and then suddenly act accordingly. It's the consistent behaviors—the hugs, the listening, the little acts of kindness—that reshape our thinking and ultimately our relationships.

Setting the Stage for Change

Instead of just hoping for better behavior, we need to create the right conditions for it. Imagine trying to get your kids to eat more vegetables by telling them to do it. That's a losing battle. But if you load the kitchen with healthy options and make sugary treats less accessible, suddenly they're munching on carrots like it's no big deal.

It's the same with relationships. Want someone to communicate more openly? Make it easy and safe for them to do so. Want more appreciation? Start by showing it yourself. The environment—both physical and emotional—has a huge impact on behavior. Set the stage for success, and the actions will follow.

Lead by Example: You Go First

Here's a cold, hard truth: waiting for the other person to change first is a recipe for disappointment. The quickest way to shift the dynamic in any relationship is to take that first step yourself. Be the one to make the first move. Show appreciation. Say thank you. Express love, even when it feels a bit awkward.

And yes, it will feel awkward at first—like trying to hug a cactus. But trust me, the more you do it, the easier it becomes. And science backs this up. Research shows that engaging in prosocial behaviors—doing kind things for others—actually increases your own happiness, regardless of the outcome.[25] So even if the other person doesn't immediately reciprocate, you'll feel better for having done it.

Regret Comes from Inaction, Not Action

The biggest obstacle to behavior change? Fear of looking foolish or vulnerable. But here's a thought: regret doesn't come from the things you tried and failed at—it comes from the things you didn't try at all. In studies of people on their deathbeds, an overwhelming 43 percent of their regrets were about relationships they didn't nurture, emotions they didn't express, and moments they didn't act on.[26]

The Nike slogan "Just Do It" couldn't be more relevant here. In relationships, action is everything. Yes, sometimes it might be a bit messy. Maybe the person won't respond how you'd hoped, but at least you'll have taken the step. And in the long run, it's the steps you took that will bring you pride—not the ones you hesitated on.

Chapter Takeaways

- Intentions are great, but actions make the difference. Behavior change leads to better relationships, not the other way around.
- Create the right environment for change. Lead by example, show up first, and set the stage for the behaviors you want to see.
- Regret lives in inaction. Take the first step, even if it feels uncomfortable. You'll be glad you did.

Exercise

Take the time below to identify one behavior in your relationships that doesn't serve you well and takes the relationship in a direction you dislike.

Current behavior that doesn't serve me well:

____

What it looks like, sounds like, feels like:

____

Ideal behavior that would serve me far better:

____

What it looks like, sounds like, feels like:

____

How can I make it a habit?

___

What proactive action can I take today?

___

Now go and do it. Don't just decide. Make it happen.

On a scale of 1 to 10, how satisfied are you with your North Star Relationship? ___

Further Readings and Resources

- ***Triggers:*** *Creating Behavior That Lasts—Becoming the Person You Want to Be*, by Marshall Goldsmith and Mark Reiter
- ***Atomic Habits:*** *An Easy & Proven Way to Build Good Habits & Break Bad Ones*, by James Clear

Section 3
ALIGNMENT

Helena Cox's Journey Toward Konnection

Helena had always been the scrappy one—the fighter. The youngest of the three, she had spent her entire life pushing against the weight of her older siblings, determined to carve her own path. So when Alex maneuvered the buyout, leaving her with nothing but a pile of cash and a boatload of resentment, she swore she would never forgive him.

She built a wall of anger so impenetrable that even her own family struggled to reach her. Her husband, Daniel, tried to reason with her. "Helena, this rage is eating you alive. You act like you lost a battle, but what if you won? What if being free of that place is the best thing that ever happened to you?"

She dismissed him at first. But late at night, when she was alone with her thoughts, she felt the weight of her own unhappiness pressing down on her. Then came the final blow: a disastrous investment in a venture meant to outshine her brother's success. Blinded by her resentment, she had ignored red flags and sunk a considerable portion of her settlement money into a deal that crumbled within months.

For the first time, she was forced to acknowledge the destructive power of her bitterness. She was tired—tired of feeling like a victim, tired of defining herself by a past she couldn't change. And now, with her financial security shaken, she realized that letting go wasn't just an option—it was a necessity.

One day, in a moment of quiet clarity, she made a choice: she would no longer let Alex dictate her emotions. She dove into the study of positivity—not the toxic kind that ignored pain, but the kind that embraced acceptance. She read about radical ownership, about how taking responsibility for one's own happiness was the ultimate form of power.

She learned to acknowledge her resentment without being consumed by it. She practiced gratitude, first begrudgingly, then sincerely. She rebuilt her friendships, opening herself up in ways she never had before. Instead of bracing for disappointment, she leaned into vulnerability. For the first time, she understood that intimacy wasn't about winning or losing—it was about showing up, fully and openly.

Her biggest test came when her father passed away. At the funeral, she saw Alex for the first time in years. He looked diminished, not just physically, but emotionally—like a man who had been devoured by his own choices. The sight of him should have ignited old fury, but instead, she felt… compassion. He had lost everything, and though he had only himself to blame, she no longer needed to punish him in her heart.

She approached Nick and Chris, the nephews she had barely known in their adult years. "You don't have to be like him," she told them. "You get to write your own story. And if you ever want to talk, I'd love to know you better."

They hugged her. And just like that, something fractured began to mend.

Years later, Helena stood in her sunlit studio, painting. She had left the corporate world and embraced her love of art. She had found peace, not because the past had changed, but because *she* had. She had learned to accept, to be vulnerable, to balance relationships without being overpowered.

And for the first time, in a long time, she felt truly free.

chapter twelve

Positivity

A pessimist sees the difficulty in every opportunity; an optimist sees the opportunity in every difficulty.

—Winston Churchill

ON A RECENT VISIT TO STARBUCKS, I noticed two friends that came in to get their morning caffeine fix. The first woman got her coffee, took a sip, and immediately grumbled, "This is not hot enough. There goes my morning!" The second woman got the same exact coffee, took a sip, smiled, and said, "Wow, delicious. I'm ready to take on the day!"

Same coffee. Different reactions. The difference? One is choosing to see the frustration, while the other sees the blessing. How often do we get stuck obsessing about the "wrong temperature" moments in our relationships? And what if we could shift our perspective to focus on what matters?

Words Are Easy; Positivity Takes Practice

We all know that person—the eternal optimist who's always seeing the silver lining. Maybe they're the ones smiling at every delay, saying, "Well, now I have more time to read!" while the rest of us are eyeing the nearest exit.

Of course, positivity isn't about pretending everything's perfect. It's not about being that person who grins through the chaos, saying, "Everything's fine!" while the metaphorical house is on fire. (No one likes the human version of a "Hang in There" cat poster.) Instead, real positivity is about choosing what to focus on—and that's where the magic happens.

The Power of Perspective: A Comical Story of Shoes and Opportunity

In business schools, there's a classic story told about Nike. In the 1980s, Nike sent two salesmen to assess the market potential in Africa. The first one came back and said, "There's no potential here. Nobody even wears shoes!" The second salesman, however, returned, beaming. "This is the opportunity of a lifetime! Nobody wears shoes—yet."

This story is a perfect example of why perspective matters. Both salesmen were looking at the same scenario, but one saw an obstacle, while the other saw endless possibility. In relationships, we're often looking at the same situation, but our interpretation can make all the difference. Do we see the challenge in every moment, or the opportunity for growth and connection?

Beware the Trap of "Naive Positivity"

Let's talk about the cult of positivity for a second—the kind where people are practically shouting, "It's fine! Everything is wonderful!" even when it clearly isn't. If you've ever tried to work through a serious issue with someone who refuses to acknowledge reality, you know how frustrating this can be.

True positivity, the kind that sustains relationships, requires balancing optimism with authenticity, recognizing the challenges but choosing to focus on what can go right. As Churchill said, seeing the "opportunity in difficulty"—not pretending difficulty doesn't exist.

Science Backs It Up: The Power of Positivity in Relationships

Let's get nerdy for a minute. Harvard professor Shawn Achor reminds us in *The Happiness Advantage* that 90 percent of our happiness is determined by how our brains process the world, not by the world itself. In other words, it's not what happens, but how we see what happens.

Here's another gem from the world of research: in a study of climbers, participants were asked to rate how steep they thought a hill was. Turns out, when standing next to a close friend or loved one, people consistently thought the hill was 20 percent less steep compared to those standing alone.[27] So not only does positivity improve our personal outlook, but our relationships can make life's challenges seem smaller. Talk about a two-for-one deal!

The Three-to-One Rule: Positivity as a Relationship Multiplier

You've probably heard that for every negative interaction in a relationship, you need at least three positive ones to keep things healthy.* This isn't just good advice; it's science. Dr. Barbara Fredrickson, in her book *Positivity*, emphasizes that to maintain thriving relationships, we need to aim for a three-to-one ratio of positive-to-negative interactions.[28]

That means that for every time you criticize your partner for leaving their socks on the floor, you need to compliment them three times (even if it's for something as simple as not losing their keys).† Failure to do so can have consequences like emotional detachment, decreased satisfaction, or chronic stress, as negativity tends to carry more weight and lead to a spiral of defensiveness.

To improve the positive-to-negative ratios in our relationships, we can use words such as:

- I appreciate it when you ______________________________.
- You did a great job on/with ___________________________.

---

* Some researchers claim that it's as high as five-to-one, as the chemical reaction to negativity is so much more powerful than positivity. And best-selling author John Gottman claims that even the five-to-one ratio is only true during a highly tense situation or amid conflict. Generally, to maintain a truly healthy relationship, the positivity-to-negativity ratio needs to be closer to twenty-to-one. Clearly, one spoonful of tar can ruin a barrel of honey!

† While aiming for a positive-to-negative interaction ratio can help, do not feel pressured (or perhaps even attempt) to track every exchange. Focus on the bigger picture. The ongoing senses of emotional safety, care, and respect are what matter most. If you have more negative interactions than usual, it may signal a need for repair, but remember, perfection is not the goal—emotional connection is.

- Thank you for ______________________________.
- I admire your ______________________________.

Do this even when your NSR isn't doing anything heroic.

And this ratio isn't just for romantic relationships. It applies across the board: friends, family, coworkers... even how we relate to ourselves.* The more we focus on positive interactions, the stronger our relationships become. This doesn't mean ignoring problems; it means choosing to invest in what's going well.

Shifting Your Perspective

Let's take a page out of Daniel Gilbert's *Stumbling on Happiness*. He found that experiences are inherently ambiguous, meaning we can interpret them in multiple ways. And we'll often do so to the detriment of a relationship.

One way to ensure a more positive view is to take ownership. As Daniel Kahneman pointed out with "The Endowment Effect," gamblers tend to feel more confident about their horses after placing bets. It's the same with relationships—when we take ownership of our role, we start to view things in a more positive light.

For example, when your kid throws a tantrum, you can either see them as "a little monster" or as "your child who's having a rough day." That shift in perspective makes all the difference in how you respond. Instead of reacting with frustration, you might meet their meltdown with patience.

---

* We forget our relationship with ourselves is the longest one we'll have, and the way we speak to ourselves requires equal sensitivity.

Practical Positivity: Easy Wins to Boost Your Relationships

Want to know how to inject more positivity into your relationships today? Here's a list of easy, proven ways to up your positivity ratio:

- **Gratitude:** Journal about the people you're grateful for and/or tell someone why you appreciate them.
- **Compliments:** It doesn't have to be big. "You are really thoughtful for picking up coffee this morning" works beautifully.
- **Acts of kindness:** Small gestures, like holding the door or sending a thoughtful text, go a long way.
- **Physical touch:** A hug, a pat on the back, or even a fist bump can strengthen your connection.
- **Exercise and meditation:** Both are scientifically proven to improve mood and outlook, which helps in all your relationships.

Positivity Is a Choice

Life's full of little frustrations. You can either let them pile up, or you can choose to focus on what's going right. Your relationships aren't going to be perfect, but you can always choose to see the opportunity in every challenge. So next time you're tempted to grumble about cold coffee or dirty dishes, try flipping the script. Your brain (and your relationships) will thank you.

Chapter Takeaways

- We need to honestly assess our challenges while maintaining optimism about our ability to overcome them.
- Positivity acts as a predictor of relationship outcomes, and the strength of our relationships impacts our overall positivity.
- Healthy and thriving relationships necessitate a minimum three-to-one ratio of positive-to-negative interactions, and there are various proactive approaches to increase positive interactions.

Exercise

Daily activity: Ask one person around you each day, "On a scale of 1 to 10, how would you rate the balance between positive and negative communication in our relationship?" If they give you less than a 9, ask, "What could I do to raise that number?"

	Score	Common Challenges	Ways to Resolve
Monday			
Tuesday			
Wednesday			
Thursday			
Friday			

Weekend activity: Write down three things you appreciate about someone you're close to, and send a quick message or video to tell them. It could be as simple as, "Hey, just wanted to say how much I appreciate your support this week. It really made a difference for me."

[**On a scale of 1 to 10, how satisfied are you with your North Star Relationship? __**]

Further Readings and Resources

- ***The Happiness Advantage:*** *The Seven Principles of Positive Psychology That Fuel Success and Performance at Work*, by Shawn Achor

chapter thirteen

Achieving Balance

Virtue is the golden mean between two vices, the one of excess and the other of deficiency.

—Aristotle

EVER TRIED RIDING A BICYCLE UPHILL with all your weight on one pedal? It's a mess—one foot's doing all the work, you're wobbling around, and it's only a matter of time before you tip over. The secret to riding uphill? Balance. You need equal pressure on both pedals, steering straight ahead, keeping your focus.

Relationships are no different. Whether it's your partner, sibling, child, or friend, keeping things balanced is key to moving forward together. Too much weight on one side? The relationship tips. Too little effort? You're not going anywhere. The question is: How should we be thinking about relationship balance?

The Goldilocks Zone of Relationships

In 1959, Su-Shu Huang, an astrophysicist, introduced the concept of the "habitable zone," which later became known as the Goldilocks zone. For life to exist on Earth, our planet has to sit in just the right spot—not too close, not too far from the sun. (Just like Goldilocks had to find the porridge and bed that were "just right" for her needs.) Move too far in either direction, and Earth turns into a giant freezer or a fiery wasteland.

The same is true for relationships. Every relationship has its "Goldilocks zone"—that sweet spot where both people's needs are being met, and the relationship thrives. Stray too far into one person's needs, and resentment builds. Neglect the relationship altogether, and it withers away. Balance is the key, and just like in space, it's about keeping things just right—not too hot, not too cold.

But unlike planetary orbits, balance in relationships isn't something that happens organically. It takes effort, awareness, and a whole lot of small adjustments to keep things from tipping one way or the other. So how do we achieve this balance?

The Four Dynamics of Relationships: Finding the Sweet Spot

Relationships, like most things in life, aren't static. They move through different stages and dynamics, depending on how the two parties interact. Think of it like a dance—you're always adjusting your steps, sometimes leading, sometimes following, but always trying to avoid stepping on toes.

To visualize the different types of relationship dynamics that demonstrate this dance—ranging from distant or smothering dynamics to lopsided or healthy ones—look at the four most common "dance moves" below.

Lopsided Dynamic

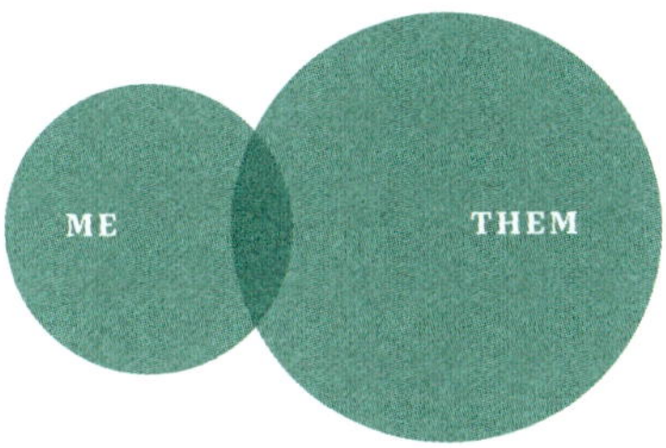

Distant Dynamic

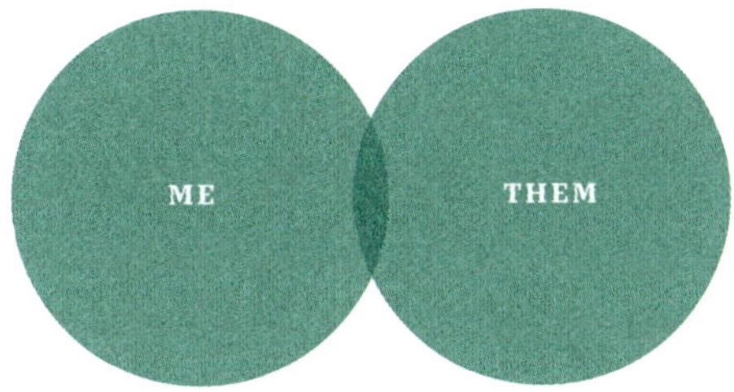

Smothering Dynamic

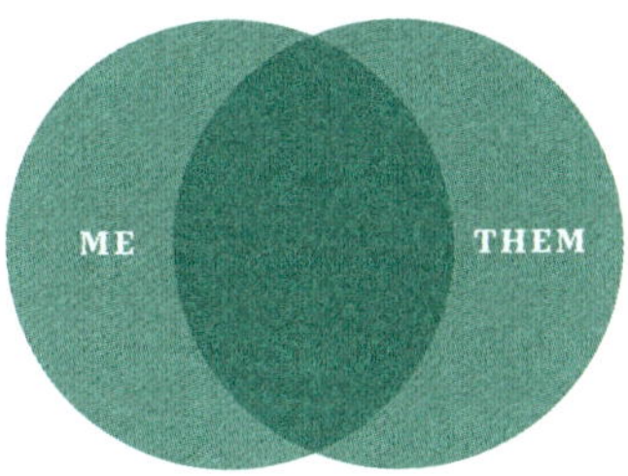

Healthy Dynamic

1. **The Lopsided Dynamic:** This is the martyr's dance. One person gives and gives, often to the point of exhaustion, while the other takes.[*] Over time, the giver grows resentful, and the imbalance becomes unsustainable.

---

[*] This may also manifest itself when one partner proactively invests in themselves, while the other is lagging (e.g., one exercises regularly and eats healthy regularly, while the other does not.) The imbalance may lead to shame, resentment, feeling "left behind" or "stuck," requiring candid conversation, support, and accommodation.

2. **The Distant Dynamic:** This is where the connection is so weak that emotional needs go unmet. Communication fizzles out, misunderstandings grow, and eventually, the members of the relationship drift apart like two boats in the fog.

3. **The Smothering Dynamic:** Ah, the classic smother. One person is so overinvested in the relationship that it suffocates the other. It's like getting a bear hug from a grizzly—you can't breathe, and after a while, you just want to escape.

4. **The Healthy Dynamic:** This is the Goldilocks zone. Both people grow individually while maintaining a strong connection. It's a partnership where support, joy, and space exist in harmony. It's not perfect, but it's adaptive.

Now here's the thing about these dynamics—they aren't set in stone. We move in and out of them. What matters is **awareness**. You need to be able to recognize when you're drifting into "lopsided" or "smothering" territory and correct course.

The Science of Balance: Meet Self-Determination Theory

To understand how to create balance in relationships, researchers Edward L. Deci and Richard Ryan introduced Self-Determination Theory (SDT).[29] According to SDT, human beings have three basic psychological needs that must be satisfied for them to thrive: competence, relatedness, and autonomy.

- **Competence:** We all want to feel like we can handle things, that we're good at what we do, and that we're capable of navigating life (and our relationships) successfully. But here's the kicker—competence isn't just about skills. It's about confidence and self-perception. Even highly capable people struggle when they doubt themselves.

- **Relatedness:** This is the glue that holds relationships together. We all need to feel connected, accepted, and like we belong. Without this sense of closeness, relationships become cold and transactional.[30]

- **Autonomy:** This is about freedom and choice. We need to feel like we're in control of our lives and decisions. Autonomy isn't about being selfish—it's about having the space to be yourself in the relationship, without feeling pressured or controlled.[31]

When these three needs are met, relationships thrive. When they're out of whack, things start to fall apart.

Spotting the Red Flags of Imbalance

How do you know when a relationship is out of balance? It's pretty simple; your red flag is **resentment**. When you find yourself begrudgingly doing things for your NSR or keeping score of who did what, you've got an imbalance on your hands.

Or maybe it's the opposite—everything feels like a transaction. "I'll do this if you do that." Relationships shouldn't be built on conditional exchanges, like some sort of emotional stock market.

When things become too transactional, what psychologists call "conditional regard," the connection becomes fragile. It's like building a house of cards—one wrong move, and the whole thing collapses.

Balancing Acts: How to Create a Healthy Dynamic

So how do you achieve balance? Through communication and cocreation. Here are some tips to help you navigate:

- **Generosity:** Give without expecting anything in return. This might sound simple, but it's incredibly powerful. Acts of kindness—whether it's making someone coffee or offering a compliment—create a positive cycle in relationships.

- **Empathy:** Take the time to understand where the other person is coming from. You don't have to agree with everything, but when people feel heard and understood, the balance automatically improves.

- **Boundaries:** Set clear, healthy boundaries and communicate them. This doesn't mean building walls—it's about making sure both people feel respected and comfortable.

- **Check-ins:** Regularly check in with each other to make sure things are on track. Balance is fluid, and without regular adjustments, you might find yourself tipping too far in one direction.

Final Thoughts: Balance Is a Moving Target

If you're thinking you can achieve balance once and be done with it—sorry, it doesn't work like that. Balance is a moving target. It requires constant tweaking, readjusting, and communicating.

Relationships are like riding that bicycle uphill. You'll wobble, you'll need to shift your weight, and sometimes you'll feel like you're not making any progress. But with each small adjustment, you get a little closer to reaching that sweet spot where both people feel seen, heard, and supported.

Chapter Takeaways

- A healthy relationship is about balance. Too much or too little of anything throws it off.
- Relationships require competence, relatedness, and autonomy to thrive.
- Resentment and transactional exchanges are signs of imbalance.
- Healthy relationships involve generosity, empathy, boundaries, and regular check-ins.

Exercise

Take a few minutes to reflect on the balance in your North Star Relationship. Complete the survey provided, and if possible, ask your NSR to do the same.* Compare your answers and start a conversation about where things are going well and where adjustments can be made. Balance is about making small shifts—not giant leaps—so start with one or two areas to focus on.

	On a positive scale of 1 to 10 (with 1 being least positive and 10 being most positive), to what extent . . .	On a negative scale of 1 to 10 (with 1 being the least negative and 10 being the most negative), to what extent . . .	Subtract the totals of the third column from the totals of the second column
Autonomy	Do I feel a sense of choice and freedom in this relationship, such that my choices reflect what I really want, who I really am, and what interests me? ____	Do I feel pressured, obligated, or even forced to engage in many activities in this relationship in ways I wouldn't have chosen to do? ______	

* The exercise was inspired by the Basic Psychological Need Satisfaction and Frustration Scale (BPNSFS), which is the primary measurement tool for assessing the level of self-determination. The actual scale is found in Appendix II.

	On a positive scale of 1 to 10 (with 1 being least positive and 10 being most positive), to what extent . . .	On a negative scale of 1 to 10 (with 1 being the least negative and 10 being the most negative), to what extent . . .	Subtract the totals of the third column from the totals of the second column
Relatedness	Do I feel that my NSR and I have warm, close, and reciprocally caring feelings in our connection together? _____	Do I feel that my NSR withholds affection, and thus is cold, distant, and superficial in their interactions with me? _____	
Competence	Do I feel confident that I can affect positive change, manage the relationship well, and achieve all my goals with it? _____	Do I question my abilities to affect positive change in this relationship and doubt my abilities to achieve all my goals with it? ____	
Total			

If the final total is 3 or lower, address the gaps immediately. If the final score is 4 to 8, develop a near-term plan to address the gaps. Higher than 8 warrants congratulations on an exceptional relationship.

On a scale of 1 to 10, how satisfied are you with your North Star Relationship? __

Further Readings and Resources

- ***Attached:*** *The New Science of Adult Attachment and How It Can Help You Find—and Keep—Love*, by Amir Levine and Rachel Heller

- ***Not Nice:*** *Stop People Pleasing, Staying Silent, & Feeling Guilty . . . and Start Speaking Up, Saying No, Asking Boldly, and Unapologetically Being Yourself*, by Aziz Gazipura

chapter fourteen

Quantity Time

You always have time for the things you put first.

—Unknown

How important is any relationship to you? Many of us hope the answer isn't correlated with the time we invest in it. And while time is rarely the sole determinant of a relationship's quality, it can serve as a simple barometer of our commitment to it.

In familial relationships, such as those between parents, adult children, and siblings, individuals can become preoccupied with their own lives, unintentionally neglecting their loved ones. Friends may allow long periods of time to pass before reconnecting with those they hold dear. Even in marital relationships, the illusion of living under the same roof can deceive us into thinking we are spending ample time together.

The Time Trap: Proximity Versus Connection

We often make the mistake of thinking proximity equals connection. Living under the same roof, sending the occasional text, or sitting through a family dinner doesn't guarantee real connection. The truth is, you can spend a lot of time physically close to someone while being emotionally miles apart.

Just think about how often you engage in conversations where you are really present. How often do you set aside uninterrupted time for meaningful interaction, not just a rushed check-in? It's easy to go through the motions without realizing that quality connection takes both time and intention.

The Myth of "Quality Time" Versus "Quantity Time"

We've all heard the argument: "It's not about quantity of time; it's about quality of time." But here's the thing—*quantity* time and *quality* time aren't mutually exclusive. You don't get one without the other. In fact, it's the regular, day-to-day investment of time that lays the foundation for deeper, more meaningful moments.

Think of relationships like gardens. You can't just water them once a month and expect them to thrive. Gardens require daily care and attention. The same goes for relationships—those fleeting, golden moments of connection don't just happen by accident. They're the result of being consistently present, showing up, and putting in the time.

Gottman's Six-Hour Rule: Turning Time into Gold

Dr. John Gottman, one of the leading experts in relationship psychology, discovered that it only takes six hours a week to maintain a thriving relationship.[32] That's right—just six hours. But here's the thing: those six hours need to be spent wisely, focusing on specific areas of connection. Gottman's Six-Hour Rule includes the following:

- **Partings:** Before leaving for the day, check in with your partner. Spend a couple of minutes asking about what's exciting or stressful in their day ahead. (Total: ten to fifteen minutes per week)

- **Reunions:** After work or at the end of the day, reconnect with a hug and a twenty-minute conversation about how the day went. (Total: 1.5 to 2 hours per week)

- **Appreciation:** Take five minutes every day to express gratitude and appreciation. Whether it's a compliment or a simple thank you, these moments of acknowledgment matter. (Total: thirty to forty minutes per week)

- **Affection:** Show physical affection daily, whether it's a hug, a kiss, or just a meaningful and thoughtful touch. (Total: thirty to forty minutes per week)

- **Date night:** Dedicate two hours a week to spending time together, doing something fun or meaningful. No distractions, just focused time. (Total: 2 hours per week)

So far, everything Gottman shared is typical, benign, and perhaps even employed loosely or religiously by countless couples. However, he adds one more dimension.

- **State of the union:** Once a week, set aside one hour to check in on the relationship. Discuss any concerns, challenges, or areas for improvement. This regular touchpoint can help prevent small issues from snowballing into bigger problems. (Total: one hour per week)

With just six hours a week, you can create a stronger, more connected relationship. While Gottman originally outlined this framework for romantic relationships, it can certainly work for other important relationships in your life—friends, siblings, parents, or colleagues.

Set aside the structured time and touchpoints. Simply reading this book will not be as effective if it is not accompanied by a commitment to spending additional time with your NSR.

Who's Getting Your Time?

We often fool ourselves into thinking that we don't have enough time. But the reality is, we always have time for the things we put first. The challenge is figuring out what—or whom—we've been putting first.

To assess your current time allocation, think about the people who have occupied most of your time this week. Did you spend meaningful time with your closest loved ones, or did your attention get pulled toward work, acquaintances, or distractions?

To answer this question, write down their names in the

quadrant that best represents their importance and frequency of interaction in your life. Consider which close relationships didn't make it into the list and whether low-importance, high-frequency contacts have monopolized your time.

	High Importance	Low Importance
High Frequency		
Low Frequency		

The Deathbed Regret Test

The common refrain is that no one on their deathbed says, "I should have spent more time in the office or scrolling social media." Instead, many express regrets for not investing more in their relationships. Now imagine you are over one hundred years old and nearing the end of your life. Complete the sentences: "I wish I'd spent more time with ________________ and less time with/on ________________." The answers can be eye-opening.

Once you've answered these questions, it becomes evident where adjustments need to be made, and where time needs to be reallocated from low-importance to high-importance relationships. Consider developing specific strategies that honor the unique dynamics of each relationship.

Rituals of Connection: How to Structure Time for Maximum Impact

Spending more time with someone doesn't mean much if the

time isn't intentional. This is where rituals of connection come in. Just like we schedule meetings or gym sessions, we should be creating rituals that ensure we're putting time into our most important relationships. For example:

- **High-importance, low-frequency relationships** (e.g., long-distance friends or family you see rarely): These relationships benefit from structured, intentional time. Plan regular calls or visits, schedule video chats, or set up a shared message group to stay connected in between in-person meetings.

- **High-importance, high-frequency relationships** (e.g., spouse, kids, or business partner): Even if you interact daily, it's crucial to schedule intentional time for deeper connection. Set up rituals like weekly dinners, monthly get-togethers, annual retreats, bedtime routines, or regular check-ins. These simple rituals create a rhythm of connection that strengthens the relationship over time.

A Simple Time Formula

In summary, to achieve balance and fulfillment in your relationships, use the following formula to assess and structure your time:

- **Evaluate the current state of your relationships:** Whom are you spending time with most often, and are they the people who matter most?

- **Shift your time toward high-importance relationships:** Can you reallocate time from low-importance, high-frequency relationships to the ones that truly matter?

- **Build rituals of connection:** Create a regular rhythm of intentional time together, whether it's through daily check-ins, weekly dates, or monthly deep dives.

Chapter Takeaways

- Quantity time matters just as much as quality time in relationships. You can't have one without the other.
- Gottman's Six-Hour Rule is a simple and effective framework to structure time for meaningful connection.
- Evaluate where your time is going. Are you giving your most important relationships the attention they deserve?
- Create intentional rituals of connection to maximize the impact of the time you spend with loved ones.

Exercise

Based on the Six-Hour Rule, create a weekly time framework for your most important relationship (your NSR). How will you incorporate partings, reunions, appreciation, and affection? When will you schedule a "state of the union" conversation to address any underlying issues?

Note: While weekly might be overkill for nonspousal relationships, all NSR relationships could benefit from a monthly or quarterly check-in. Similarly, you may not need a daily structured touchpoint, especially if your current touchpoints are highly irregular. In that case, perhaps just sending a monthly text message is a significant step forward. Either way, think about it, write it out, and schedule it!

Sun	Mon	Tues	Wed	Thur	Fri	Sat

On a scale of 1 to 10, how satisfied are you with your North Star Relationship? __

Further Readings and Resources

- ***The Seven Principles for Making Marriage Work:*** *A Practical Guide from the Country's Foremost Relationship Expert*, by John Gottman, PhD, and Nan Silver

- ***The Relationship Cure:*** *A 5 Step Guide to Strengthening Your Marriage, Family, and Friendships*, by John Gottman, Ph.D., and Joan DeClaire

chapter fifteen

Intimacy

We cultivate love when we allow our most vulnerable and powerful selves to be deeply seen and known.

—Brené Brown

ACCORDING TO DATING SITE EHARMONY, a study on one thousand Australian couples revealed that relationships go through five stages: the spark phase, the honeymoon phase, the intimacy phase, the commitment phase, and, sadly, the heartbreak phase.[33] However, the criteria they used to define "intimacy" might raise an eyebrow or two. Apparently, a relationship reaches peak intimacy when both parties can say "I love you," pass gas in front of each other, and forgo makeup. Yes, flatulence and bare faces are now the hallmarks of closeness. Is this really what intimacy has been reduced to? Surely, it's more than bodily functions, some superficial words, and skipping foundation.*

So what exactly is intimacy, and how do we cultivate it in a way that moves beyond gas and cosmetics?

The Four Types of Intimacy: More Than Just Comfort

Intimacy is often oversimplified, but it's much richer than just sharing life's little quirks. To break it down, let's start by recognizing that intimacy comes in four flavors:

- **Emotional intimacy:** Being present, supportive, and open to each other's emotions, allowing for raw, honest communication without fear of judgment.

- **Physical intimacy:** This can be as simple as casual hugs, kisses, or even pats on the back but may also include more intense sexual touches in romantic relationships. Ultimately, it's about the comfort and warmth we derive from touch when we are physically together.

- **Intellectual intimacy:** Sharing ideas, thoughts, and opinions openly. It's having deep conversation where you feel connected on a mental level, whether you agree or not.

- **Spiritual intimacy:** This one's a bit more abstract, but it's about feeling united in your journey, your values, or even

* The superficiality of these indicators aside, the culmination of these five stages being the "heartbreak phase" made the study far less inspiring and/or useful (notwithstanding the reality that most relationships don't last).

shared beliefs. It's where you connect with someone on a higher plane—think purpose, faith, or common life goals.

The best relationships encompass all four types of intimacy, though few manage to balance them perfectly. If you're not there yet, don't worry. You're not alone. The good news is that improving one or two of these types can massively enhance your connection.

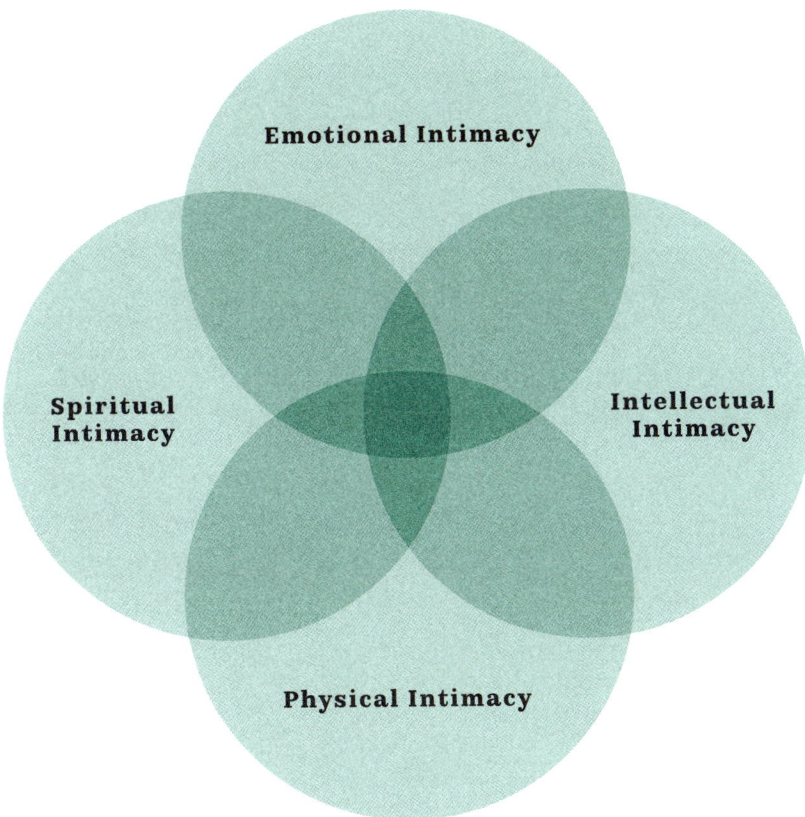

The Vulnerability Factor: Into Me, You See

Achieving intimacy, no matter the type, boils down to one thing: vulnerability. (Spoiler alert: It's scary, but it's necessary.) If we want deep connection, we must be willing to show parts of ourselves that we'd rather keep hidden. As cheesy as it sounds, intimacy is basically short for "Into me, you see."

Think about it, how easy is it to talk about the weather, work, or your favorite TV show? Super easy. But how comfortable are you sharing your hopes, fears, insecurities, or that embarrassing story from middle school? Probably not so much.

It's this discomfort that keeps us skimming the surface with our relationships. We're so used to small talk and jokes that we forget to dive deeper into the things that really matter—like values, emotions, or the core of who we are. And the sad part is, if we don't dig below the surface, we miss out on being fully understood and loved for who we truly are.

The Cultural Iceberg: What You See Is Only 10 Percent

Anthropologist Edward T. Hall introduced the Cultural Iceberg Model in the 1970s, which compared the self we show the world to an iceberg.[34] Only about 10 percent of who we are is visible to others, while the remaining 90 percent is hidden beneath the surface. What's above the waterline is often a carefully crafted version of ourselves—the polished bits we feel comfortable displaying to the world.

The challenge is that the stuff lurking below the waterline is way more important. That's where our real thoughts, feelings, beliefs, and vulnerabilities lie. If we never let anyone glimpse below that 10 percent, we're not really letting people know us at all.

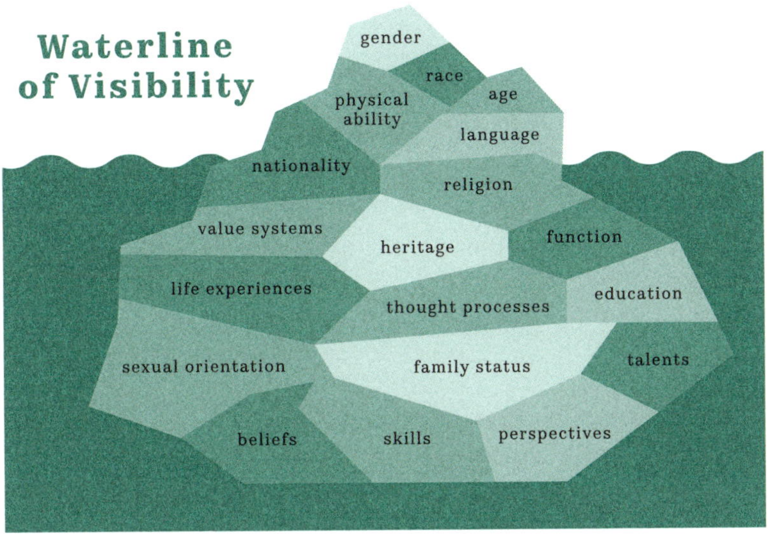

To establish intimacy, we must be willing to reveal aspects of ourselves that we may fear showing the world, and even admitting these aspects to ourselves. For instance, we might feel comfortable engaging in casual conversations about sports, weather, or factual data. However, when it comes to sharing our thoughts, views, and judgments, we may feel uneasy. Similarly, we may be comfortable expressing our thoughts and ideas, but struggle to share our deepest feelings. Alternatively, we might feel open about our emotions but hesitant to disclose our deepest desires.

Virtual Lives, Cropped Selves

As if it wasn't hard enough to reveal ourselves in the real world, the virtual world makes it even trickier. Now, instead of 10 percent visibility, we're cropping even more of our true selves out of the frame. Social media lets us curate an idealized, filtered version of life. But connection doesn't happen through filters—it happens when we allow people to see us as we are, unfiltered, with all the awkwardness and imperfections that come with it.

The virtual world gives us the illusion of connection, but intimacy requires more than likes, comments, or heart emojis. If we don't risk being vulnerable, we miss the chance to be accepted, and even celebrated, for who we are. And in a world where everyone's trying to be picture perfect, real connection comes from showing up, mess and all.

The Intimacy Equation: Vulnerability + Time = Connection

Building intimacy is like a slow burn—it doesn't happen overnight, and it doesn't happen without effort. The real work begins when we decide to let people in. It's about risking awkwardness, potential rejection, or embarrassment to share the parts of ourselves that we usually keep hidden. It's about showing up, being honest, and inviting someone to truly see you. And the payoff? A deeper, more fulfilling relationship.

Chapter Takeaways

- There are four main types of intimacy: emotional, physical, intellectual, and spiritual.
- True intimacy requires vulnerability—being willing to share the hidden 90 percent of who you are.
- The more of ourselves we hide, the less connected we become to others.
- The virtual world can make intimacy even more challenging by distorting how we present ourselves.

Exercise

Practice building intimacy by playing the "If you really knew me . . ." game with your NSR or someone you want to get closer to. Start by sharing something from just beneath the surface, such as a belief, value, or experience you typically keep private. For example, "If you really knew me, you'd know that I'm terrified of public speaking, even though I do it for a living." Take turns, choosing two to three topics each. Vulnerability begets vulnerability.

[On a scale of 1 to 10, how satisfied are you with your North Star Relationship? __]

Further Readings and Resources

- ***Hold Me Tight:*** *Seven Conversations for a Lifetime of Love*, by Dr. Sue Johnson.
- ***Daring Greatly:*** *How the Courage to Be Vulnerable Transforms the Way We Live, Love, Parent, and Lead*, by Brené Brown

chapter sixteen

Extreme Ownership

Between stimulus and response, there is a space. In that space is our power to choose our response. In our response lies our growth and our freedom.

—Viktor Frankl

WE'VE ALL BEEN THERE—something goes wrong in a relationship, and what's the first thing we think? "It's their fault." They said the wrong thing, did the wrong thing, didn't do enough of the right thing. And while that might be factually true, here's the kicker: playing the blame game never actually fixes anything. Blaming someone else for how you feel just hands over all your power to them—and who really wants to give away control like that?

The Secret to Stronger Relationships: Owning Your Emotions

Here's the thing: owning your emotions doesn't mean pretending everything is fine or brushing off how you feel. It means recognizing that, while you can't always control what happens to you, you can control how you respond. You have a choice in how you handle situations, and that choice directly shapes the future of your relationships.

Think of it this way: when you hand over responsibility for your emotions to someone else, you're basically letting them steer the ship. If they're not invested in the journey, or if they're dealing with their own storm, you could end up off course. Owning your emotions means taking back the wheel—and steering yourself in a better direction.

Emotions Are Neither Good Nor Bad; They Just Are

Here's a common mistake: we judge our emotions. We feel anger, disappointment, or jealousy, and immediately we think, "I shouldn't feel this way. Something's wrong with me." But emotions aren't good or bad—they just are. The key isn't to suppress them but to recognize them, understand them, and accept them. Sometimes, the best thing you can do to fully process a feeling is give yourself twenty-four hours, sleep on it, and see how you feel afterward.

Think about the last time you were really upset. Maybe it felt huge in the moment, but by the next morning, it seemed a little more manageable. That's because the neural processing of emotions is intense in the moment but tends to fade.[35] Once you've given yourself some space, then you can start taking action—calmly, rationally, and without blaming others for what's going on inside you.

Extreme Ownership: It's Not About Blame; It's About Power

Now here's where things get interesting. Owning your emotions is great—but there's another level: responsibility. Not only can we recognize how we react, but we can also look back and say, "How did I contribute to this situation?" This is where extreme ownership comes in.

Best-selling authors Jocko Willink and Leif Babin talk about this concept in their book *Extreme Ownership*, which is all about strengthening our internal locus of control—focusing on what we can do, instead of what others should have done. It's the idea that most things in life happen because of our actions (or inaction), and our future is shaped by the choices we make now.

Does that mean we're responsible for everything that happens? No. But we are responsible for how we show up, how we react, and how we shape our relationships moving forward.

A New Way to Think About Responsibility

Willink and Babin break down responsibility into four levels:

	Actions	Emotions
Individual Responsibility	**Level 1: Individual Responsibility** Taking responsibility for your actions.	**Level 2: Emotional Responsibility** Taking responsibility for your emotions when they show up in interactions with others.
Collective Responsibility	**Level 4: Extreme Ownership** Taking responsibility for other people's actions and how those made others feel.	**Level 3: Complete Ownership** Taking responsibility for how your actions made others feel.

Here's the kicker: complete ownership (level 3) doesn't mean you take the blame for everything. And the concept of *extreme ownership* is not totally practical or healthy in various relationship contexts—since it can be harmful for us to own other people's emotions—but it challenges us to stretch our imaginations.

The notion of extreme ownership compels us to consider what else we could do to make others feel safer or more comfortable. It prompts us to consider what more we could have done for our NSR. It's not about determining who is "right" or "wrong." It's certainly not intended to place unrealistic standards on us, and it's important not to confuse *complete ownership* with insecurity or extreme guilt. Its value is in recognizing your role in the relationship and asking, "What could I have done better?" You can't control how others react, but you can control how you contribute to the situation—and that can make all the difference.

Imagine a World of Complete Ownership

Just imagine a world where everyone took complete ownership. Conflicts wouldn't escalate, frustrations wouldn't turn into blame fests, and misunderstandings would be met with empathy, not defensiveness. It's not about being perfect—it's about showing up and doing your part to make things better.

Here's the reality: not everyone's ready for complete ownership. Some people have fragile egos or aren't prepared to take responsibility for their own lives, let alone anyone else's. But even if the people around you aren't fully there, you can set the tone by embracing ownership yourself. When you stop blaming others, you'll be amazed at how your relationships change for the better.

Ownership ≠ Micromanagement

Let's clear something up: ownership doesn't mean micromanaging other people's lives or controlling every aspect of the relationship. It's about empowering yourself to create better circumstances and outcomes. It's about being proactive rather than reactive.

At the end of the day, even strained relationships aren't inherently bad relationships. Sometimes they just need some management, and the more ownership you take, the more influence you have to turn things around.

Chapter Takeaways

- We control how we respond. Our emotions don't control us—we control what we do with them.
- Ownership opens up new possibilities. When we take responsibility for our relationships, we can change how they evolve.
- Complete ownership is a game changer. It's about acknowledging that we've played a role in the current state of the relationship—and recognizing that we have the power to change it.

Exercise

Consider a few recent stresses or arguments with your NSR. Outline the emotions that you felt:

What prompted the feelings?

How did you respond?

____

____

If you took full responsibility for those emotions, what could you have done differently?

____

____

If you took more ownership of this relationship, how might you have approached the situation such that those emotions never even surfaced (e.g., planning, communication, discipline)?

____

____

How will you improve that in the future?

____

____

On a scale of 1 to 10, how satisfied are you with your North Star Relationship? __

Further Readings and Resources

- ***You Can't Make Me Angry,*** by Dr. Paul O.
- ***Extreme Ownership:*** *How U.S. Navy SEALs Lead and Win,* by Jocko Willink and Leif Babin

chapter seventeen

Acceptance

Emotional maturity demands ongoing, total acceptance of people, places, things, and situations as they are, rather than as I might wish them to be.

—Dr. Paul O.

PICTURE YOURSELF ON YOUR FIRST MORNING of the beach vacation you've been eagerly anticipating. You're about to walk outside, beach ready, for a day of sun and relaxation, and it starts to pour. You could curse the weather, shake your fist at the clouds, or even pack up and leave. Or—you could grab an umbrella, feel the rain on your skin, and choose to enjoy the sounds of the waves in a new way. The rain doesn't change your day, but how you respond to it does. Welcome to the power of acceptance.

Acceptance isn't about liking the rain, the difficult person in your life, or the mess your lazy brother leaves behind. It's about understanding that life—and people—aren't here to meet your expectations. They just are. And your happiness? That depends less on changing others and more on accepting what's in front of you, warts and all. We often don't get to pick the hand we're dealt, but we do choose how we play it. Acceptance is about learning to work with the hand we have, even when it's not the one we wanted.

Embracing the Chaos: Acceptance in Real Life

We've all been there—feeling frustrated, disillusioned, or disappointed in a relationship because people don't always live up to our imagined standards. But they're not supposed to. And that's where acceptance comes in.

Acceptance doesn't mean you're blind to someone's flaws, or that you love everything about them twenty-four seven. It means recognizing that the person in front of you is a whole, imperfect human being. They're going to do things that bug you. They're going to have quirks, bad habits, and rough edges. And your job? To decide whether those imperfections are deal-breakers—or just the price of admission for the relationship you actually want.

Marcus Aurelius: The OG of Acceptance

Take a page out of Marcus Aurelius's book. For the Roman emperor and revered philosopher, acceptance was among the four biggies—his four pillars of stoic philosophy. Aurelius famously said, "I'm going to be meeting people today who talk too much—people who are selfish, egotistical, ungrateful. But I won't be surprised or disturbed, for I can't imagine a world without such people."[36]

Despite his immense power, he did not impose his will on

those who differed from him. He accepted people as they were, earning the trust and respect of millions in the process. Now if a guy who ran an entire empire could accept that not everyone is going to be a ray of sunshine, maybe we can cut our friends, partners, and families a little slack too.

The Five Ways We Deal with Relationship Frustrations

Psychologist John Thoburn, an expert in family psychology, breaks down our typical responses[37] when we hit those bumps in the road:

1. **Tolerate:** You grit your teeth and endure it—simmering quietly with resentment but never saying anything.

2. **Retaliate:** You go on the offensive or withdraw, emotionally or physically, as a means of expressing your dissatisfaction.

3. **Manipulate:** You guilt-trip, shame, or use fear to get your way.

4. **Negotiate:** You try to strike a deal—"I'll put up with this if you put up with that."

5. **Relate:** The gold standard. You accept people as they are, quirks and all.

The goal? Move from tolerating or retaliating to relating. Accepting others for who they are doesn't mean you love every little thing about them. It means you acknowledge their full humanity and work with, not against, their differences.

There's a Big Difference Between Tolerance and Acceptance

Let's get one thing straight: acceptance and tolerance are not the same thing. Acceptance is peaceful. Tolerance is . . . well, putting up with something while secretly wishing it would change.

Acceptance	Tolerance
At peace with what is	Willingness to let it continue
Leads to appreciation without judgment	Requires teeth-gritting restraint to ignore
Feelings of freedom and softening	Feelings of entrapment and tension
No desire to change the other person	Endure pain while trying to change
Willingly celebrating the differences	Indulging others with grudging resignation
Fosters greater understanding/intimacy	No context for differences

Acceptance is about finding freedom in what is, rather than fighting to change the unchangeable. It's about making peace with the quirks, the differences, and even the frustrations that come with being in any relationship—romantic, familial, or otherwise.

Relationships Are About Navigating Differences, Not Erasing Them

The reality is that every relationship comes with differences. Even identical twins raised together aren't clones of each other. And that's okay. Maybe one is a morning person and one a night owl. Maybe one is a planner, and one is more spontaneous. It's not important who's right and who's wrong; rather, it's how you make those differences work for you instead of against you. The key isn't to wish away the differences, but to figure out how to navigate them.

Also, consider that two people who are exactly alike aren't necessarily better than total opposites. Similarities can cause the same tensions as differences. For instance, two people who share the same interests may lack variety and stimulation, or two individuals with identical personalities may clash. Therefore, it is not the differences and similarities themselves that determine the success of a relationship, but rather the judgments and perspectives we hold about those differences and similarities.*

The Myth of Endless Options

In today's world, it's easy to fall into the trap of thinking there's always something (or someone) better out there. With dating apps and social media, it's tempting to believe happiness is just one click or swipe away. Everyone else's family seems more functional. Everybody else's partners, bosses, and employees seem so nice.

---

* The exception to this rule would be any moral, ideological, and value-based differences. These can be major impediments to long-term relationships and need to be carefully considered in advance, as having completely different values is likely to compromise mutual respect and will be generally more difficult to accept.

The sad irony is that the more options we have, the less satisfied we become. It's called the paradox of choice,[38] and it's real.

The truth is, relationships aren't about finding someone perfect. They're about building something meaningful with someone imperfect—just like you. And the more we focus on accepting the person in front of us, rather than idealizing someone else, the deeper and more fulfilling our relationships become.

It Starts with Self-Acceptance

As we saw with emotional fluency, we must start closer to home. To accept others, you first have to accept yourself. Ever notice how the things that bug you the most about other people often reflect the things you struggle with in yourself? That's not a coincidence. When we're secure in our own skin, it's a lot easier to give others grace for their imperfections. Self-love leads to acceptance—and that acceptance will extend outward to our NSR.

Chapter Takeaways

- There are five ways we respond to frustration: tolerate, retaliate, manipulate, negotiate, or relate. Relating is the key to healthy, lasting relationships.
- Acceptance is about celebrating differences without trying to change the other person.
- We have the power to decide whether our differences will create conflict or connection.
- Self-acceptance is the first step to accepting others.

Exercise

Practice acceptance with your NSR. Start by listing what makes them great. Outline their traits that inspire your love for them. What makes them great and particularly special to you?

Now tackle what drives you nuts. Outline their quirks, idiosyncrasies, and differences that you've historically found frustrating.

Why do these things bother you? What's underneath your frustration? Be honest, but without judgment. Stick to the facts.

Why do the good traits outweigh the annoying ones? Reflect on why it's worth accepting the quirks. Why do those quirks pale in comparison to the traits that make the individual special to you?

What opportunities do their differences present? Consider how their unique traits and idiosyncrasies actually add to your relationship or life.

Make an affirmation statement. What kind of verbal affirmation can you create to serve as a balancing reminder when frustration with your NSR kicks in? For example, "*Yes, my partner's tendency to leave socks everywhere drives me crazy, but I accept them for who they are because their thoughtfulness in other areas means more to me than a spotless house.*"

[On a scale of 1 to 10, how satisfied are you with your North Star Relationship? __]

Further Readings and Resources

- ***The Gifts of Acceptance:*** *Embracing People and Things as They Are*, by Daniel A. Miller
- ***ACT with Love:*** *Stop Struggling, Reconcile Differences, and Strengthen Your Relationship with Acceptance and Commitment Therapy*, by Dr. Russ Harris

Closing Thoughts

First of all, congratulations! You've made it through volume 1, Committed Connections, and that's no small feat. You've taken the first steps toward strengthening the most important relationships in your life. So go ahead; take a moment to celebrate your progress. Yes, right now. If this was a physical book, I'd suggest a victory lap around the house, book in hand. Because here's the truth: you're already on the way to building deeper, more meaningful connections.

Now let's be honest: your work doesn't stop here. This is just the beginning, and there's so much more in store. But here's the good news: the tools you've developed in this first volume are not just theories. They are action-oriented, and the sooner you start applying them, the quicker you'll see results. So why wait? Take what you've learned and get to work today—because nothing changes until you take that first step.

As we saw with the collapse of Cox Industries, the separation of the Cox siblings had nearly destroyed them, but for Caroline and Helena, it also became their greatest catalyst for growth. They had taken different paths than Alex, Caroline toward mastery of communication and Helena toward mastery of self, though both had arrived at the same place: a life richer in connection, built not on resentment, but on intentional, committed relationships. And in the end, that was the true legacy they left behind.

So let's quickly summarize what we've achieved and recap some of the key insights from volume 1:

- **Relationships are the essence of life:** at the end of the day, nothing will matter more than the quality of our connections. Whether it's your family, dear friends, or any other North Star Relationship, the depth of these bonds is your greatest investment. Start with self-awareness—because, as Carl Jung taught us, self-discovery is the foundation of any healthy relationship. Without it, you're just shooting arrows in the dark.

- **Set realistic expectations:** no relationship is perfect (news flash, right?). It's okay to have goals and aspirations for your connections, but remember—progress beats perfection every time. Track your wins, celebrate the small victories, and stay motivated. Even two steps forward and one step back is still progress.

- **Shared purpose fuels lasting relationships:** whether you're Marie and Pierre Curie discovering radium, or just trying to survive Monday morning school drop-offs, aligning on a shared purpose strengthens commitment and resilience. As the African proverb reminds us, "If you want to go fast, go alone. If you want to go far, go together."

- **Trust is the cornerstone:** trust isn't just about competence—it's about integrity, reliability, and understanding. As Warren Buffett wisely said, "It takes twenty years to build a reputation and five minutes to ruin it." Relationships are no different. Be both trustworthy and trusting. When trust is solid, even the small bumps in the road feel manageable.

- **Master emotional fluency:** let's face it; emotions run the show. Becoming emotionally fluent means recognizing both your own emotions and those of the people around you—and reacting in ways that build bridges instead of walls. It's like Virginia Satir asked: "Do you want to be right, or do you want to be married?" (Hint: Winning the argument is overrated when any connection is on the line.)

With these tools, you're equipped to start making meaningful changes in your relationships. Just remember, relationships aren't static—they're living, breathing things that need constant care, attention, and action.

So what's next? Volume two! In the next leg of our journey, we're diving into the art and science of Caring Communication. Because let's face it: relationships live or die based on how we communicate. And spoiler alert: most of us have a lot to learn.

But for now, pause, reflect, and put some of these ideas into practice. Trust me, the ripple effects will surprise you.

Until volume two . . . keep making your relationships the masterpiece of your life.

[On a scale of 1 to 10, how satisfied are you with your North Star Relationship? __]

Appendix I

The Relationship Assessment Scale

The Relationship Assessment Scale (RAS)[39] was developed by researcher Susan Hendrick as a brief but reliable scorecard for NSR relationships. While there are numerous tools for assessing relationships, many are time-consuming and most suitable for romantic couples. The RAS focuses on measuring global relationship satisfaction, and works for a broader range of relationship types. It consists of seven items, each rated on a five-point scale. The brevity of the scale increases its utility in clinical settings, and research has shown the scale to be correlated with other measures of love, trust, and commitment.

To complete the RAS exercise, please circle the letter (A/B/C/D/E) that best answers each question for you.

1. How well does this individual (i.e., your NSR) meet your needs?				
A	B	C	D	E
Poorly		Average		Extremely well

2. In general, how satisfied are you with your relationship?				
A	B	C	D	E
Unsatisfied		Average		Extremely satisfied

3. How strong is this relationship compared to most?				
A	B	C	D	E
Poor		Average		Excellent

4. How often do you wish you didn't have this relationship?				
A	B	C	D	E
Never		Average		Very often

5. To what extent has your relationship met your original expectations?				
A	B	C	D	E
Hardly at all		Average		Completely

6. How much do you love and appreciate your partner?				
A	B	C	D	E
Not much		Average		Very much

7. How many problems are there in your relationship?				
A	B	C	D	E
Very few		Average		Very many

To score the assessment, convert the letters to numbers, with the values being commensurate with the number, and add them up. Though, here's the tricky part. For questions 1, 2, 3, 5, and 6, the scoring is A=1, B=2, C=3, D=4, E=5). And for questions 4 and 7, the numbers are scored in reverse order (A=5, B=4, C=3, D=2, E=1).

List your scores below:	
Q1	
Q2	
Q3	
Q4	
Q5	
Q6	
Q7	
Total	

Scores of 7 to 14 suggest low satisfaction in your relationship. Scores of 15 to 21 suggest average satisfaction, and scores of 22 to 35 indicate a high level of satisfaction.

Appendix II

Basic Psychological Need Satisfaction and Frustration Scale[40]

IN THE FOLLOWING PAGES, we ask you about the kind of experiences you actually have in your life. Please read each of the following questions carefully. You can choose from 1 to 5 to indicate the degree to which the statement is true for you at this point in your life.

Please respond to each statement by indicating how true it is for you. Use the following scale.

1	2	3	4	5
Not true at all				**Very true**

1. I feel a sense of choice and freedom in the things I undertake. ____

2. Most of the things I do feel like "I have to." ____

3. I feel that the people I care about also care about me. ____

4. I feel excluded from the group I want to belong to. ____

5. I feel confident that I can do things well. ____

6. I have serious doubts about whether I can do things well. ____

7. I feel that my decisions reflect what I really want. ____

8. I feel forced to do many things I wouldn't choose to do. ____

9. I feel connected with people who care for me and for whom I care. ____

10. I feel that people who are important to me are cold and distant toward me. ____

11. I feel capable of what I do. ____

12. I feel disappointed with many of my performances. ____

13. I feel my choices express who I really am. ____

14. I feel pressured to do too many things. ____

15. I feel close and connected with other people who are important to me. ____

16. I have the impression that people I spend time with dislike me. ____

17. I feel competent to achieve my goals. ____

18. I feel insecure about my abilities. ____

19. I feel I have been doing what really interests me. ____

20. My daily activities feel like a chain of obligations. ____

21. I experience a warm feeling with the people I spend time with. ____

22. I feel the relationships I have are just superficial. ____

23. I feel I can successfully complete difficult tasks. ____

24. I feel like a failure because of the mistakes I make. ____

Total ____

Scoring information:

Scores are determined by averaging subscale scores for questions as indicated below.

Autonomy satisfaction: questions 1, 7, 13, 19

Autonomy frustration: questions 2, 8, 14, 20

Relatedness satisfaction: questions 3, 9, 15, 21

Relatedness frustration: questions 4, 10, 16, 22

Competence satisfaction: questions 5, 11, 17, 23

Competence frustration: questions 6, 12, 18, 24

Appendix III

Key Terms and Concepts

Acceptance (versus tolerance): Tolerance is the ability or willingness to endure something, while acceptance moves past that and promotes an environment of equity, mutual respect, and appreciation.

Conditional regard: A transactional approach, where approval, affection, or love are offered based on whether a person meets specific expectations or behaviors. It means valuing someone only when they behave in desired ways, which can lead to feelings of pressure, insecurity, or diminished self-worth in the person receiving the conditional regard.

Dunning-Kruger effect: A cognitive bias in which people with limited competence overestimate their own abilities.

Emotional intelligence: The capacity to be aware of, control, and express one's emotions and to handle interpersonal relationships with a good sense of judgment and empathy.

Endowment effect: Describes how individuals place more value in items they own, than they would if the item did not belong to them.

Extreme ownership: Using elevated responsibility to place the fate and future of our relationships in our hands.

False narratives: Beliefs based on incorrect or incomplete information.

Johari's window: A framework for thinking about self-awareness through insight into different aspects of our identity.

Maslow's hierarchy: Five-level model of human needs, depicted in a pyramid. One typically needs to satisfy the lower needs before they can attend to the higher needs. From bottom up, the needs are: basic physiological needs (food, water, shelter), safety and security needs (job, health, protection), love and belonging needs (family, friends, community), self-esteem (confidence, achievement, respect), and self-actualization (purpose, creativity, morality).

North Star Relationship (NSR): Refers to the individual(s) with whom you most want to enhance your relationship. This could include a family member, spouse, friend, colleague, or others.

Offers (versus requests): A request is typically a demand for something, while an offer is to give or present something. Unlike requests, offers hold intrinsic value for the individual.

RACI matrix: Responsible, Accountable, Consulted, Informed. This matrix outlines the different parties involved in decision-making: those responsible for the work, those with final authority, those whose input is sought, and those who need to be kept informed.

Realistic expectations: Having conservative and sensible expectations that factor in human frailty, imperfections, communication gaps, and the unexpected, to mitigate the prospect of being disappointed by reality.

Safety: Trust that we can feel emotionally secure with another person.

Secondary emotions: Emotional reactions we have that tend to follow our initial, visceral emotions.

Self-determination theory: A theory introduced by Edward Deci and Richard Ryan that refers to a person's ability to make choices and manage their life. The theory suggests people can become self-determined when their need for competence, relatedness, and autonomy are fulfilled.

Shared purpose: Aligning on a shared purpose to rise above mundane challenges and stresses of everyday life.

Trigger: An event or situation which causes someone to do something or potentially causes distress.

Waterline of visibility: Aspects of a person that we can see but may or may not see accurately due to assumptions we make about appearances.

Wheel of emotions: A visual representation of primary emotions, which helps people put a name to specific emotions while considering varying nuances and complexities, helping one develop greater self-awareness.

Appendix IV

Sources and References

1. Scherwitz, L., L. E. Graham 2nd, G. Grandits, J. Buehler, and J. Billings. "Self-Involvement and Coronary Heart Disease Incidence in the Multiple Risk Factor Intervention Trial." *Psychosomatic Medicine* 48, no. 3–4 (1986): 187–99. https://doi.org/10.1097/00006842-198603000-00004.

2. Byington, R. P. "Beta Blocker Heart Attack Trial: Design, Methods, and Baseline Results. Beta Blocker Heart Attack Trial Research Group." *Controlled Clinical Trials* 5, no. 4 (1984): 382–437. https://doi.org/10.1016/s0197-2456(84)80017-3. PMID: 6151483.

3. Berkman, Lisa F., and S. Leonard Syme. "Social Networks, Host Resistance and Mortality: A Nine Year Follow Up Study of Almeda County Residents." *American Journal of Epidemiology* 109, no. 2 (February 1979): 186–204. https://doi.org/10.1093/oxfordjournals.aje.a112674.

4. Holt-Lunstad, Julianne, Timothy B. Smith, and J. Bradley Layton. "Social Relationships and Mortality Risk: A Meta-Analytic Review." *PLOS Medicine* 7, no. 7 (July 2010): e1000316. https://doi.org/10.1371/journal.pmed.1000316.

5. Valtorta, N. K., M. Kanaan, S. Gilbody, S. Ronzi, and B. Hanratty. "Loneliness and Social Isolation as Risk Factors for Coronary Heart Disease and Stroke: Systematic Review and Meta-Analysis of Longitudinal Observational Studies." *Heart* 102, no. 13 (2016): 1009–1016. https://doi.org/10.1136/heartjnl-2015-308790. Interestingly, the nature of relationships (whether social, familial, or communal) mattered less than the relationships' strength and authenticity. Furthermore, individuals with strong relationships outlived those with better health but weaker ties.

6. Easterlin, Richard. "Paradox Lost?" *Review of Behavioral Economics* 4, no. 4 (2017): 311–339. https://doi.org/10.1561/105.00000068.

7. Mineo, Liz. "Good Genes Are Nice, but Joy Is Better." *Harvard Gazette*, April 11, 2017. https://news.harvard.edu/gazette/story/2017/04/over-nearly-80-years-harvard-study-has-been-showing-howto-live-a-healthy-and-happy-life/.

8. "Study of Adult Development." Harvard Second Generation Study. Accessed June 24, 2025. https://www.adultdevelopmentstudy.org/.

9. Waldinger, Robert J., and Marc S. Schulz. "What's Love Got to Do with It? Social Functioning, Perceived Health, and Daily Happiness in Married Octogenarians." *Psychology and Aging* 25, no. 2 (2010): 422–31. https://doi.org/10.1037/a0019087.

10. Mogilner, Cassie. "The Pursuit of Happiness: Time, Money, and Social Connection." *Psychological Science* 21, no. 9 (2010): 1348–54. https://doi.org/10.1177/0956797610380696.

11. Ungerböck, Krister. 22 *Talk Shifts: Tools to Transform Leadership in Business, in Partnership and in Life*. Lioncrest Publications, 2020. See p. 22.

12. "The Transition of the Family Business." *Fraser Blog*, October 11, 2016. https://www.fraserlawfirm.com/blog/2016/10/the-transition-of-the-family-business/.

13. National Park Service. "We Have Met the Enemy and They Are Ours." U.S. Department of the Interior, April 20, 2016. https://www.nps.gov/articles/met-the-enemy-4.htm. Accessed February, 9, 2025.

14. Joy, Melanie. *Getting Relationships Right: How to Build Resilience and Thrive in Life, Love, and Work*. Berrett-Koehler Publishers, 2020.

15. Flaum, J. P. "When it Comes to Business Leadership, Nice Guys Finish First." Green Peak Partners, n.d. https://greenpeakpartners.com/wp-content/uploads/2018/09/Green-Peak_Cornell-University-Study_What-predicts-success.pdf.

16. Luft, J., and H. Ingham. "The Johari Window, a Graphic Model of Interpersonal Awareness." *Proceedings of the Western Training Laboratory in Group Development* (1955). University of California, Los Angeles.

17. Harkin, Benjamin, Thomas L. Webb, Betty P. I. Chang, et al. "Does Monitoring Goal Progress Promote Goal Attainment? A Meta-Analysis of the Experimental Evidence." *Psychological Bulletin* 142, no. 2 (2015): 198–229. https://doi.org/10.1037/bul0000025.

18. *Journal of Family Psychology* by A.I. Luskin and colleagues (2007); *Journal of Social and Personal Relationships* by J.H. Harvey and colleagues (2007); *Journal of Social and Personal Relationships* by R.A. Neff and J.A. Karney (2003).

19. Stone Zander, Rosamund, and Benjamin Zander. *The Art of Possibility: Transforming Professional and Personal Life*. Penguin, 2002.

20. Perel, Esther. "Why Modern Love Is So Damn Hard." *Esther Perel* (blog), n.d. https://www.estherperel.com/blog/why-modern-love-is-so-damn-hard.

21. Villamizar, Gabe. "Simon Sinek - Trust Vs Performance (Must Watch!)." Posted November 17, 2022. YouTube. https://www.youtube.com/watch?v=PTo9e3ILmms.

22. Sweeney, Patrick J., Kurt T. Dirks, David C. Sundberg, and Paul B. Lester. "Trust The Key to Leading When Lives Are on the Line." *US Army Research* 356 (2011). http://digitalcommons.unl.edu/usarmyresearch/356.

23. Benson, Kyle. "Reaching a Compromise: The Second Part of the State of the Union Meeting." The Gottman Institute. June 23, 2017. https://www.gottman.com/blog/reaching-compromise-second-part-state-union-meeting/.

24. Dunning, D., and J. Kruger. "Unskilled and Unaware of it: How Difficulties in Recognizing One's Own Incompetence Lead to Inflated Self-Assessments." *Journal of Personality and Social Psychology* 77, no. 6 (1999): 1121–1134. https://doi.org/10.1037/0022-3514.77.6.1121.

25. Dunn, E. W., L. B. Aknin, and M. I. Norton. "Spending Money on Others Promotes Happiness." *Science* 319, no. 5870 (March 2008): 1687–8. https://doi.org/10.1126/science.1150952. Erratum in: *Science* 324, no. 4932 (2009): 1143. PMID: 18356530.

26. Morrison, M., and N. J. Roese. "Regrets of the Typical American: Findings From a Nationally Representative Sample." *Social Psychological and Personality Science* 2, no. 6 (2011): 576–583. https://doi.org/10.1177/1948550611401756.

27. Schnall, S., K. D. Harber, J. K. Stefanucci, and D. R. Proffitt. "Social Support and the Perception of Geographical Slant." *Journal of Experimental Social Psychology* 44, no. 5 (2008): 1246–1255. https://doi.org/10.1016/j.jesp.2008.04.011.

28. Fredrickson, Barbara. *Positivity: Top-Notch Research Reveals the 3-to-1 Ratio That Will Change Your Life*. Harmony, 2009.

29. Deci, Edward L., and Richard M. Ryan. *Intrinsic Motivation and Self-Determination in Human Behavior*. Springer, 1985.

30. Deci, E. L., and R. M. Ryan. "The 'What' and 'Why' of Goal Pursuits: Human Needs and the Self-Determination of Behavior." *Psychological Inquiry* 11, no. 4 (2000): 227–268. https://doi.org/10.1207/S15327965PLI1104_01.

31. Deci, E. L., and R. M. Ryan. "Autonomy and Need Satisfaction in Close Relationships: Relationships Motivation Theory." In *Human Motivation*

and Interpersonal Relationships: Theory, Research, and Applications, edited by N. Weinstein. Springer Science + Business Media, 2014. https://doi.org/10.1007/978-94-017-8542-6_3.

32. Gottman, John M., and Nan Silver. *The Seven Principles for Making Marriage Work*. Harmony Books, 1999.

33. Dunn, Billie Schwab. "EHarmony Research Reveals What People Do in a Relationship." Mail Online. Daily Mail. December 7, 2017. https://www.dailymail.co.uk/femail/article-5157587/eHarmony-research-reveals-people-relationship.html.

34. Hall, Edward T. *Beyond Culture*. Anchor Books, 1976.

35. Lindquist, K. A., T. D. Wager, H. Kober, E. Bliss-Moreau, and L. F. Barrett. "The Brain Basis of Emotion: A Meta-Analytic Review." *Behavioral and Brain Sciences* 35, no. 3 (2012): 121–143. https://doi.org/10.1017/S0140525X11000446.

36. Aurelius, Marcus. Meditations. Translated by George Long. Penguin Classics, 2002.

37. Thoburn, John. "Acceptance: The Foundation of Lasting Relationships." *Psychology Today*. December 10, 2012.. https://www.psychologytoday.com/ca/blog/he-saidshe-said/201212/acceptance-the-foundation-lasting-relationships.

38. Pilat, Dan, and Sekoul Krastev. "The Paradox of Choice." The Decision Lab. 2021. https://thedecisionlab.com/reference-guide/economics/the-paradox-of-choice.

39. Hendrick, S. S., Dicke, A., & Hendrick, C. (1998). The Relationship Assessment Scale. *Journal of Social and Personal Relationships*, 15(1), 137-142. https://doi.org/10.1177/0265407598151009 (Original work published 1998)

40. Van der Kaap-Deeder, J., B. Soenens, R. M. Ryan, and M. Vansteenkiste. "Manual of the Basic Psychological Need Satisfaction and Frustration Scale (BPNSFS)." Ghent University, Belgium, 2020; Chen, B., J. Van Assche, M. Vansteenkiste, B. Soenens, and W. Beyers. "Does Psychological Need Satisfaction Matter When Environmental or Financial Safety are at Risk?" *Journal*

of Happiness Studies 16 (2015): 745–766. https://doi.org/10.1007/s10902-014-9532-5; and Chen, B., M. Vansteenkiste, W. Beyers, et al. "Basic Psychological Need Satisfaction, Need Frustration, and Need Strength Across Four Cultures." *Motivation and Emotion* 39 (2015): 216–236. https://doi.org/10.1007/s11031-014-9450-1.

About the Authors

BORN IN UKRAINE, MO LIDSKY'S entrepreneurial journey spans seven countries and multiple industries such as automotive, finance, nonprofit, real estate, and technology. Today, Mo serves as the chairman and CEO at Prime Quadrant, as well as director and officer on several corporate and charitable boards. Mo has authored several acclaimed books, including *The Philanthropic Mind, In Search of the Prime Quadrant,* and *Selling Snake Oil.* Drawing from years working closely with ultra-affluent families, Mo's books are intended to help families improve their financial, social, and human capital. The konnect better initiative resulted from the recognition that no amount of financial assets could replace (or acquire) our most cherished relationships and the deep, loving connections we yearn for. As a result, Mo has focused this new book on empowering families to strengthen the relationships that matter most, as that is where true wealth ultimately lies.

Bob Gould is a partner at Creaghan McConnell Gould Ltd. As the overseer of CMG's Family Capital Services division, he has carefully selected a team of highly talented professionals from across North America. He and his team focus on how relationships and financial planning affect the outcome the family is striving for.

Bob is dedicated to supporting one of Canada's most valuable resources—the country's top business families. For over thirty years, he has paid attention to the best practices that successfully support their unique ownership challenges: estate, succession, and exit planning. Bob has also supported many of Canada's best advisors as they assist these families.

What Bob has learned is that the technical part of planning is so important to do thoughtfully, recognizing that it will continue to evolve as life changes. More important, however, is paying attention to what really matters to the family and how relationships can either support or undermine a very well thought out plan.

konnectbetter.com
/Konnect Better
@KonnectBetter
@konnectbetter